The
MID-WALES
RAILWAY

by
R.W. Kidner

THE OAKWOOD PRESS

© Oakwood Press 1990

ISBN 0 85361 406 7

Typeset by Gem Publishing Company, Brightwell, Wallingford, Oxfordshire.
Printed by Alphaprint, Witney, Oxfordshire.

All rights reserved. No part of this book may be reproduced or transmitted in any form or by any means, electronic or mechanical, including photo-copying, recording or by any information storage and retrieval system, without permission from the Publisher in writing.

Acknowledgments

Information and assistance has been received from many people over the past 30 years since my first book on the Cambrian Railways was published. For this present work I wish especially to acknowledge the assistance of the following: D.S.M. Barrie, R.E. Thomas, Elwyn Jones, Dr Stewart Jones, Gwyn Brianant-Jones, C.C. Green, W.D. Hines, Bill Giles, W.M. Faulknall, and the staff of the National Library of Wales, Aberystwyth, who have provided access to many maps and manuscript collections which were vital to an accurate coverage of some difficult facets of a complex history.

R.W.K
1990

Bibliography

Top Sawyer, Ivor Thomas, Longmans 1938
The Cambrian Railways, Miller & Christiansen, David & Charles 1979
Mishaps on the Cambrian Railways, Elwyn Jones, Severn Press 1972
The Hay Railway, C.R. Clinker, David & Charles 1960
The Brecon & Merthyr Railway, D.S.M. Barrie, Oakwood Press 1980 edition
The Manchester & Milford Railway, J.S. Holden, Oakwood Press 1979
North Wales Branch Album, C.C. Green, Ian Allan 1983
The Railway Magazine, especially 1906 Vol. XVIII, p. 419 (Central Wales Railway); September 1938, p. 203 (Railways in the Wye Valley); June 1951 p.361 (Talyllyn Junction).
The Locomotive Magazine, September 1913 to August 1914, (Cambrian Railways Locomotives).

Published by
The OAKWOOD PRESS
P.O.Box 122, Headington, Oxford.

Contents

The train arrival hand bell from Talgarth station (*left*) and the arrival bell from Builth Road station (*right*). Both bells were photographed in 1930.

Courtesy Welsh Industrial and Maritime Museum, Cardiff

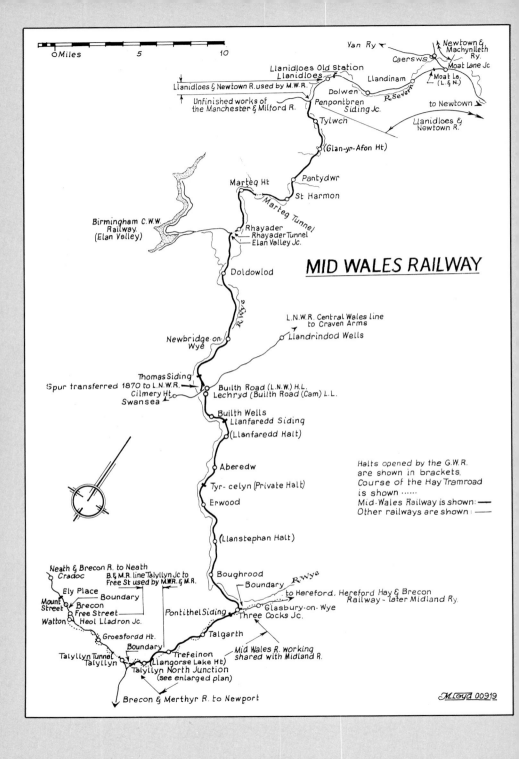

Introduction

The boundaries of Mid-Wales are not fixed, but it is generally regarded as containing the old counties of Radnor and Cardigan, with the north part of Brecknock and Carmarthen, and the south part of Montgomery. It differs from north and south Wales in that the former is associated with slate quarrying, and the latter with coal and iron, whereas Mid-Wales is agricultural where it is not barren. It is especially difficult for communications because of extensive mountain areas north of the Ystwyth Valley and north-west of Rhayader. Before the railways there was a weekly stage coach from Machynlleth via Llanidloes and Rhayader to Presteign and New Radnor. There was also one running from Brecon up to Llandrindod Wells; but no coach crossed the whole area from north to south.

Because of its lack of minerals and large towns, railway promoters tended to regard Mid-Wales as something to be got through, either from England to the coast, or from north to south Wales. This was not the view locally; on the occasion of the opening of the Llanidloes & Newtown Railway, the *Shrewsbury Chronicle* wrote:

> Mid-Wales . . . entirely devoid of railway communications, notwithstanding that this district is the seat of large flannel and woollen manufacturing, contains many towns of importance, that its mineral wealth is boundless . . . that it has on its coast harbours of world-wide celebrity — let us hope that every man feeling an interest in Wales will never rest until his native soil is riddled with railways.

Before long the soil of Mid-Wales was certainly riddled with proposed railways, and these have perforce been recited, hopefully in a way which does not become tedious. It should also be said that a railway which did not own either of its termini is likely to have complex relationships; the Mid-Wales was in physical contact with five other railways, and meddled in the affairs of others. These stories have all been told, in places at the expense of chronology. The Mid-Wales was born in a short period of Welsh railway mania, mostly locally-inspired. Had the rivalry between the Great Western and the London & North Western been less bitter, no doubt one or other of them would with a broad sweep have made all the muddle of the 1860s unnecessary. But it did not happen, and so the complex web of some score of railways in the area, actual or constructed, must be unravelled.

R.W. Kidner
1990

A construction train at Llanelwedd, just south of Builth Wells. The locomotive is thought to be ex-Newcastle & Carlisle Railway *Venus* built by Thomas Bros. in 1841, or possibly R. & W. Hawthorn in 1836.

Courtesy A. Skidmore

Chapter One

The Battle of the Acts

Railway promoters were at work in the 1840s planning lines from the north-west manufacturing areas across Mid-Wales to the South Wales ports. One such in 1845 was the Manchester & Milford Railway; this failed, though a company of the same name was closely embroiled in our story later on. Railways from England to the coast were also proposed; however the Shrewsbury & Aberystwyth Railway of 1852 also failed. The North & South Wales Railway of 1850 was planned in two sections, one from Manchester to Llanidloes, and the other from there to Milford Haven. In fact most schemes saw Llanidloes as the gate through which they must pass, because of the difficult country to the west of it.

The Rev. Samuel Roberts of Llanbrynmair wrote in 1854 that Montgomeryshire 'could boast the loveliest homes for Peers of the Realm, and had sea-lords, bank-lords, game-lords and coach-lords, but no railways'. He saw Newtown as a railway metropolis with tentacles stretching in all directions, and in fact within six years of writing his speech, Newtown did have three railways, running to the west, north and south. That to the south, the Llanidloes & Newtown, opened first and was entirely isolated. The two big English companies, the Great Western and the London & North Western, had both applied for Acts in the area in 1853, but had lobbied against each other, so that only the local line got its Bill, with no connections to Shrewsbury or elsewhere being approved.

The railway was the brain-child of one G.H. Whalley, a landowner from near Ruabon, who had attempted to become MP for Montgomeryshire, but instead had to accept the seat at Peterborough, though this did not restrain him from being active in railway promotion in Mid-Wales. He also promoted the Oswestry & Newtown Railway, and claimed in his prospectus that by affiliation with the Oswestry & Chester Junction Railway, and an extension southwards to Carmarthen and Milford Haven, this would provide a direct route for the New York passenger traffic. It was not the last time that these mythical American tourists and business men would be heard of, but in fact most people were thinking of moving cotton products southwards and coal northwards.

Whalley was not the only player in the field; two others were David Davies of Llandinam and Thomas Savin. The former had been a top sawyer in a timber mill and a small farmer, but his organising ability, together with an uncanny knack of costing railway cuttings by just looking at the land, made him a railway promoter and contractor with few equals, who promoted and partly financed most of the railways in Mid-Wales. He was later a big coal-owner in South Wales. Savin was a different kind of man, a draper by trade, a self-taught railway promoter-cum-contractor; he was possessed of great ambition but not too much judgment. The two had joined up to build the Vale of Clwyd Railway at the request of one Benjamin Piercy. However, their partnership was to be brief; Davies became frightened of Savin's extravagant schemes and was lucky to get his assets out of the partnership before the latter crashed. Piercy was a locally-born engineer who had irons in many fires; although he spent many years railway-building

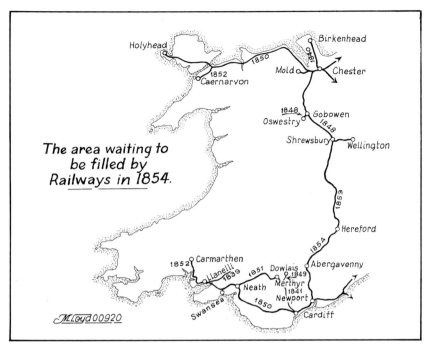

The area waiting to
be filled by
Railways in 1854.

The Cambrian Railway Sharp, Stewart 'Queen' class, 0–6–0 *Cambria* seen here at
Machynlleth about 1875. The Mid-Wales Railway locomotives Nos. 9 and 10 (*1872
numbering*) were of this class.   *Author's Collection*

abroad, his opinions always counted in the Cambrian Railways counsels; judging from the correspondence of his which has survived, he was a clear thinker and full of common sense.

The route later taken by the Mid-Wales Railway (MWR) was described in a provisional prospectus of a railway titled 'The Llanidloes & South Wales Railway Co. Ltd'. The only copy available is undated, but appears to have been put out in 1857. It is extremely well-written, and makes a passionate appeal for local people to do something constructive; it attacks the 'gigantic projects that have brought discredit upon Railway Enterprises in this district'. This may be a reference to the abortive attempts of the two big companies, the Great Western and the London & North Western, or possibly to the ridiculously inflated proposals such as that to build an 'atmospheric' railway from Gloucester to Aberystwyth. In promising gradients no worse than 1 in 100 it ignores geography, and in saying that seaborne trade in copper and coal from Swansea to Liverpool 'must hereafter use this line' it is too hopeful.

> The object of the undertaking, [it states] is to proceed to the completion of the Main Trunk Line of Railway from Swansea, Llanelly and Milford to Manchester, Liverpool and the North of England. Leaving the railway now in course of construction at Llanidloes, it follows the valley of the Dulas Brook to Pen-y-pont-bren, then turning by Tylwch it passes Pantydwr and St Harmon villages, and along the valley of the Marteg to the junction of that river with the Wye. Proceeding down the Wye Valley it passes through Rhayader, entering Breconshire near the junction of the rivers Wye and Elan, continuing thence on the Breconshire side of the former river to Newbridge.

The line terminated at Newbridge, the prospectus said, because a railway was projected from the Shrewsbury & Hereford line via Newbridge and Llandovery 'from whence a line is in course of construction to the existing Llanelly Railway'. This is a reference to a railway being promoted westward from Leominster, which in fact never got further than Kington. 'American and other foreign trade cannot much longer find sufficient accommodation in Liverpool' we are told, 'and where else is there a satisfactory substitute than Milford Haven'. The Oswestry & Newtown Railway (O&N) 'is about to be made' and the railway offered in this prospectus was a better prospect, for the O&N would have to share its traffic with the canal. The writer was Richard Wood, a Rhayader solicitor; no Directors were mentioned, though 'landowners through whose land the railway will pass are most favourable'.

In March 1859 a meeting was held under the chairmanship of Mr Whalley of what was known as 'the Mid-Wales section of the Manchester, Liverpool, Swansea & Milford Haven Junction Railway'; a map had been circulating showing the route as given above, but going on to Llandovery, and with a branch line from Newbridge to Llandrindod Wells. However at the same time meetings were going ahead to plan what would become the Central Wales Railway (CWR) which started at Craven Arms on the Shrewsbury & Hereford and was aiming for Llandovery via Llandrindod Wells and Llangammarch Wells. Both the Mid-Wales and Central Wales put in Bills, but both were abridged by Parliament; the former to Newbridge and the latter to Llandrindod Wells.

The Act enabling the railway with the now-shortened title of 'Mid-Wales Railway' to construct a line from Llanidloes to Newbridge-on-Wye was passed in August 1859; it was to be the first of many.

While the Mid-Wales had made modest progress at its northern end, the shape of things at what would be its southern end was still wrapped in obscurity; the hope was still for Llandovery, but another possibility was emerging. The town of Brecon was the terminus of the Brecknock & Abergavenny Canal; it had originally been intended to go on to Newbridge-on-Wye, but in fact it had stopped at a basin on the southern outskirts of Brecon. Now there were two railways aiming for the town also; the Brecon & Merthyr Tydfil Railway (B&M), and the Breconshire Canal & Railway Co., proposing, in effect, to convert the canal into a railway.

The centre of activity was the office of Brecon solicitors Maybery, Williams & Cobb, and much of what ensued can be read in the remaining 'Maybery Papers', though matters were actually handled by J.N. Cobb, with one eye over his shoulder at local banker J.P. de Winton. The position in 1858 was that the two companies had realised the folly of having the same route into the town from Talybont, and had come together to see whether the trains of one could use the metals of the other. Agreement seemed close, though the canal company refused at first to allow the other company, known locally as 'the Merthyr' to share in any profit made on the joint route. This seemed to have been ironed out, and when the Brecon & Merthyr Bill was read for the first time, the section between Talybont and Brecon was omitted. Then in early 1859 the canal company unexpectedly pulled out, too late for the other participant to rewrite its Bill.

Brecon was also the target for the Hereford, Hay & Brecon Railway (HH&B), formed in 1857. Its station in that town was to be in the north, with the intention of going on to Swansea or Milford Haven. The undertaking was beset by problems and made slow progress; in 1859, hearing that the ancient tramroad from Eardisley to the canal basin of the Brecknock & Abergavenny Canal at Brecon was for sale, the HH&B decided to buy this to get into Brecon and abandon its north route through Bronllys. This move caused concern to the Mid-Wales and the Brecon & Merthyr; the former was considering running to Brecon if the route to Llandovery was lost, while the latter needed this entry to make good its loss of the powers from Talybont. A good deal of pressure was exerted in Parliamentary circles, and when the HH&B Bill was approved in 1860 it was agreed that the company would allow its rivals to purchase the tramroad east of Glasbury (Three Cocks), though it was granted running powers into Brecon. It was not done without tears; at one point the Mid-Wales bought a large parcel of shares in the Hay Railway to try to frustrate the HH&B, but failed.

It is hard to tell at this point who was really stirring the pot. Two letters have been preserved with a bearing on matters. One was from Savin to Cobb written in October 1859, suggesting joining up the Oswestry & Newtown, Llanidloes & Newtown, Mid-Wales, and a relaid tramroad into Brecon. The other was written by Benjamin Piercy in November, from 'The Great Western Royal Hotel, London Terminus' also to Cobb, advising him that powers would now be sought for railways from Newbridge to Llandrindod

ANNO VICESIMO SECUNDO & VICESIMO TERTIO

VICTORIÆ REGINÆ.

****

Cap. lxiii.

An Act for making a Railway from *Llanidloes* in the County of *Montgomery* to *Newbridge* in the County of *Radnor,* to be called " The *Mid-Wales* Railway;" and for other Purposes.

[1st *August* 1859.]

WHEREAS the making of a Railway from the *Llanidloes and Newtown* Railway at *Llanidloes* in the County of *Montgomery* to *Newbridge* in the County of *Radnor* would be great local and public Advantage: And whereas the Persons hereinafter named, with others, are willing at their own Expense to carry such Undertaking into execution: And whereas it is expedient that the *London and North-western,* the *Great Western,* the *Birkenhead, Lancashire, and Cheshire Junction,* the *Oswestry and Newtown,* the *Llanidloes and Newtown,* the *Shrewsbury and Welchpool,* and the *Newtown and Machynlleth* Railway Companies, and the Company incorporated by this Act, and in this Act called "the Company," should be enabled to enter into Working and Traffic Arrangements as herein-after mentioned: And whereas the Objects aforesaid cannot be effected without the Authority of Parliament: May it therefore please Your Majesty that it may be enacted; and be it enacted by the Queen's most Excellent Majesty, by and with the Advice and Consent of the Lords Spiritual and

[*Local.*]   10 *C*   Temporal,

The front page of the 1859 Mid-Wales Railway Act.

Wells, Builth Wells, and Llandovery; and from Builth Wells to Three Cocks and Talyllyn; this would be entitled the 'Breconshire, Radnorshire & Carmarthen Junction (Mid-Wales) Railway Act'. Since he made no mention of Brecon, and nobody would terminate a railway at Talyllyn, it seems a deal must have already been done to give the route west of there to the B&M.

Some detailed planning must have taken place, for there is also preserved a Petition from a gentleman in Llandovery against 'the Mid-Wales Railway being built through my land'.

The meticulous plans for the Breconshire, Radnorshire ad Carmarthen Jn Railway (BR&CJR) drawn up in Piercy's office in Welshpool still exist, and show some difference from the details in the letter quoted above. The line started with a junction with the approved route of the Central Wales Railway south of Llandrindod, and ran just south of the town of Newbridge, with a junction with the Mid-Wales Railway. Two miles further on there was a triangular junction with a branch southwards to Builth. Further west, near what was later Garth station, a branch line ran north from Maescefnyffordd to Allt-y-Dinas, up the Dulas Valley (not the same Dulas as the former Tylwch) for 5½ miles; its purpose was to serve some mines. The railway ended with an end-on junction with the Towy Valley at Llandovery. None of these lines were built as such; the Mid-Wales used a differing route when it built south to Builth, and the Central Wales took a somewhat less direct route between Llandrindod and Llanfairfechan, resulting in the junction with the Mid-Wales being at Llechryd and not just south of Newbridge.

The year 1860 was a pivotal one for the Mid-Wales, for in that Parliamentary session both the Mid-Wales and Central Wales put in again for a line to Llandovery, and a Parliamentary Committee having sat on the matter, granted that route to the Central Wales Extension Railway (CWER). The Central Wales was at this time in three parts, the Knighton Railway from Craven Arms, the Central Wales to Llandrindod Wells, and the CWER from there to Llandovery; for simplicity it will all be referred to as the Central Wales. The line was opened from Llandrindod Wells on 1st November, 1866 to Builth Road (adjoining the Mid-Wales Llechryd station). Local service began from Garth, the next station west, on 11th March, 1867, according to an account by the booking clerk there given many years later, who said that a large number of tickets were sold on that day to Builth Wells market. Services reached Llanwrtyd on 6th May and Llandovery on 1st June, 1868.

It is worth remembering that from Llandovery down to Swansea the whole line was at that time in the hands of the Llanelly Railway (LR) but from 1868 its lease of the Vale of Towy Railway (Llandovery–Llandilo) was shared with the Central Wales, and in 1871 the portions of the LR between Llandilo and Carmarthen and Pontardulais and Swansea (Victoria) were taken over by the LNWR, who had also taken over the CWR in 1866. The remaining parts of the Llanelly Railway went to the Great Western, who thereby also took over a share in the working of the former Vale of Towy. All this has been detailed because otherwise what follows might be somewhat confusing.

Although it means jumping ahead in time, the upshot of the LNWR triumph in 'getting' Llandovery rather than it going to the Mid-Wales must

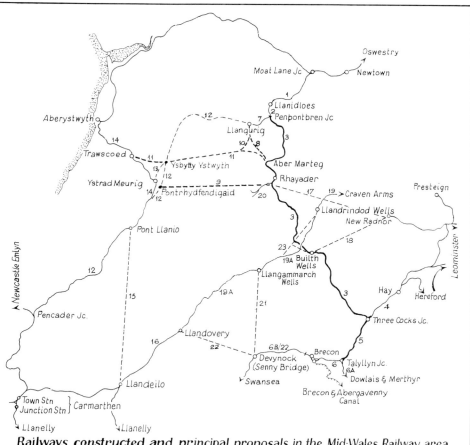

Railways constructed and principal proposals in the Mid·Wales Railway area.

Proposed lines are shown conventionally, no attempt is made to plot the proposed route.

- 1. Llanidloes & Newtown Railway (L.&N.)
  2. L.&N. Joint line for the M.W. & M.&M.R.'s
- 3. Mid·Wales Railway (M.W.R.)
- 4. Hereford, Hay & Brecon Railway (H.H.&.B.R.) used by Midland Ry.
  5. H.H.&.B.R. owned by M.W.R.
  6.   "   "   by B.&M.R.
- 6A Brecon & Merthyr Ry. (B.&M.R.)
- 6B Neath & Brecon Ry. (N.&.B.R.)
  7. Constructed part of the M.&M.R. 1860 line
  8. { M.&M.R. Rhayader Branch. 1861.
       { M.W.R. Llangurig Branch. 1863.
  9. "   Aberystwyth Branch. 1861.
  10. "   Llangurig Branch. 1865.
  11. "   Western Extension 1865.
- 12. Manchester & Milford Ry. (M.&M.R.) Main Line 1860.

13. M.&M.R. Ysbytty Ystwyth Branch 1865.
14.   "   Deviation 1864.
15. Swansea & Aberystwyth Junction Ry 1864
16. Vale of Towy Ry.
17. Worcester-Aberystwyth Ry. 1872.
18.   "   "   "   "   1876.
19. Central Wales Ry.
19A. Central Wales Extension Ry.
20. Elan Valley Ry.
21. N.&.B.R. Senny Bridge & Llangamarch Branch.
22. Brecon & Llandovery Junc. Ry 1865
23. Brecon, Radnor & Carmarthen Junc. Ry 1859

For explanation of abbreviations refer to those marked •

M.Lloyd 00921

be followed through. The South Wales Railway had built from Chepstow through to Narberth Road in Pembrokeshire and was hesitating over its last step to Milford Haven. The Carmarthen & Cardigan Railway was building north from the first-named towards Pencader; both these lines were broad gauge. The Vale of Towy had been open since 1858 and as stated the CWR had a share in this, though in its 1859 Act the Mid-Wales also had an agreement with the Vale of Towy. Away to the west was another interesting railway, the Pembroke & Tenby. This had David Davies on the Board, and later one John Barrow who was the main financier of the Manchester & Milford Railway (M&M). In fact the two companies were virtually amalgamated, though separated by some 30 miles of broad gauge track between Whitland and Pencader.

The LNWR was determined to reach Milford Haven, and obtained running powers over the Carmarthen Junction Railway to just north of that town, and ran into it over the Carmarthen & Cardigan, by now standard gauge. From here the P&T had forced the Great Western to convert one line to Whitland to 'mixed'; running powers were granted to the LNWR (though the P&T had signed an agreement with the Mid-Wales in 1865) and by 1869 through coaches were running from Manchester and Liverpool into Tenby. They had done it; Manchester to Milford Haven! But the victory was short-lived; the Great Western had bought the South Wales in 1863 and was mopping up all the lines; from 1872 trains from Tenby to Carmarthen were cut back to Whitland. There were to be no more through LNWR coaches from Manchester or Liverpool. All the great area of the Milford Haven would become GWR territory: Milford, Neyland, Pembroke dock, later Fishguard. However, the LNWR was prepared for this; it had secured running powers over the Llanelly Railway from Llandilo to Pontardulais and leased the line from there into Swansea. Through coaches could still run over the Central Wales, but not to the Haven.

It follows from the above that the Manchester & Milford Railway also missed out; from 1872 their trains from Aberystwyth had to terminate at Pencader. How the Mid-Wales would have fared had they got to Llandovery can now only be guessed at.

Before returning to 1859 and the actual building and running of the line, there are some other Parliamentary matters to be mentioned. In 1861 the Mid-Wales prepared a Bill for its most ambitious branch line. This would have started with a triangular junction south of Rhayader, at what was later Elan Valley Junction, and run up the Elan and Claerwen Valleys; the mountains would be tunnelled to reach the Teifi Valley and the comparatively easy country north of Tregaron Bog used to reach the Ystwyth Valley, to run with the river into Aberystwyth. The line of the Manchester & Milford Railway as then approved crossed this route at Pontrhydfendigaid. This route was not entirely impracticable, and would have been strategically useful in giving a direct line from South Wales into Aberystwyth (which at that time the Manchester & Milford was not planning); but it would have meant a stretch of some 10 miles from its Rhayader end with no station, for the area was almost totally unpopulated and remained so. The cost frightened the Board, and they dropped it.

The 1862 Act empowered some deviations of route near Builth, and making a junction with the intended Central Wales Extension Railway at Llechryd (later Builth Road). In fact the Mid-Wales was below the Central Wales here and the junction was in the form of a spur line, not opened until 1866, and then for goods only; it was transferred to the LNWR in 1870.

For the Mid-Wales the intrusion of the Central Wales was both a good and a bad thing; it would bring some traffic via the junction, but would also tap off some traffic from the Newbridge area. The attitude of the Board was ambivalent, but after the battle for Llandovery was lost it seems to have settled in favour of co-operation. The Rev. H. Bold writing to friends about a meeting in the committee room of the House of Lords, at which he was present in June 1861, reported that when the proposal was put that the Mid-Wales would not oppose the Central Wales Extension 'Lords Powis, Vane and Sudeley, Sir Watkin Williams-Wynn, General Wood and Mr Piercy were all in favour'. A salvo of guns comprising two Earls, a Baron, and three other men of influence would have silenced any opposition. Sir W. William-Wynn, although his 'seat' was in the north at Wynnstay, carried weight locally because he owned land near Machynlleth also, and was a director of O&N and the Newtown & Machynlleth Railway.

Of two Acts in 1863, the first was mainly financial; the second, the Mid-Wales (Llangurig Branch) Act, authorised a branch line from Aber Marteg near St Harmon to Llangurig, to which the Manchester & Milford Railway was now building. This would have allowed traffic from the Carmarthen area to run to Rhayader; however changed circumstances led to this Act being abandoned in 1865, as detailed later.

Meanwhile the rails over which traffic from the north would come down were being completed. Goods traffic began on the Llanidloes & Newtown on 30th April, 1859, and passenger traffic on 31st August. Trains began to work right through from Oswestry to Newtown on 10th June, 1861. The former was of course already linked to the GWR; however, the further Cambrian link to Whitchurch opened on 27th July, 1864. The joint line from Shrewsbury to Buttington Junction for Welshpool opened on 27th January, 1862. Thus all these places now had communication with Chester and Shrewsbury, exciting still further the promoters of lines to the south. The Llandiloes & Newtown was given a connection to the west by the Newtown & Machynlleth, which branched off it at Moat Lane, on 3rd January, 1863 and the first section of the line onwards to Aberystwyth opened a few weeks later; an amazing change in just a few years, but the fact remained that southwards Llanidloes was the end of the line.

It was not, of course, going to stay that way for long. Mention has already been made of the fact that the Mid-Wales Aberystwyth branch would have crossed over the original Manchester & Milford Railway main line, which was to run from Llanidloes via Llangurig to Pencader. The Mid-Wales Railway line as described also left Llanidloes southwards, and when both Acts were passed, Parliament failed to note that both were on the same route for 1½ miles. The Mid-Wales offered the M&M the use of their works, but the offer was refused, as was the obvious counter-offer. There was the prospect either of rival gangs of navvies getting in each others' way, or of both projects being held up for lack of agreement. In the end the problem was solved by the Llanidloes & Newtown Railway (L&N) offering to build the line to the point of divergence, and to lease it jointly to the two companies; the Act that enabled this oddly forbade the L&N to work over its own line; it would simply collect 5 per cent of capital cost in rent.

The L&N set about building a double line southwards from the site of its proposed joint station to serve three railways, to Penpontbren, a lonely spot above the Dulas River, where the M&M crossed over it by a high arch bridge, while the Mid-Wales followed it on the east bank. It was not a junction in the ordinary sense, since the two rails did not connect with each other; it was however, the point of junction between the Cambrian (as the L&N became) and the Mid-Wales. (The belief that the latter began at Llanidloes is still alive, and surfaced as recently as 1989 in an article in the *Cambrian News*.) It was no disgrace for a railway to begin or end so; it was always said that the Great Northern Railway 'ended in a ploughed field', and so it did. But it was a pity that the Mid-Wales's situation at Penpontbren was mirrored at its southern end. To paraphrase Oscar Wilde, to lose one terminus may be described as a misfortune, but to lose both begins to look like bad management.

The M&M branch was constructed as far as Llangurig, but the continuation through a long tunnel and on to Trawscoed and Pencader was never completed.

The decision to build a railway over the route of the old Hay Tramroad has been mentioned above. An Act of 1860 allowed the Mid-Wales to build south to meet the Hay at what was later Three Cocks Junction, and the various discussions which ended in the Hereford Hay & Brecon Railway route being cut into three parts were ratified by Parliament. The Mid-Wales would have the part between Three Cocks (Glasbury) and the east end of Talyllyn tunnel, the Brecon & Merthyr would have the tunnel and the line into Brecon, while the HH&B would retain the part between Hereford and Glasbury.

M. W. R.

Llanidloes to

Brecon

Chapter Two
Construction and Opening

For the sake of clarity, the various Mid-Wales Railway Bills up to 1863 have been cited in the previous chapter, but we must now go back to 1859, when on 2nd September the first sod of the railway was cut near Rhayader by Mrs Pyne of Doldowlod Hall. This was a curiously muted affair, compared with that of the Oswestry & Newtown Railway, at whose sod-cutting the great guns of Powis Castle boomed forth, and a service was taken by an Archdeacon. But in its own way it was exciting, for the timing had been inopportune. Mr Whalley had just been voted from the Chairmanship by friends of Davies and Savin, and he held court in a marquee, making trenchant criticisms of the way in which this pair financed their railway activities. The *Shrewsbury Chronicle* gleefully reported the mayhem; one of Mr Whalley's more quotable statements was that 'he was a gentleman and an MP, and it was not his place to argue with contractors'. There were supporters on both sides, and the waiters were sufficiently worried by the catcalls and hisses to remove from the tables anything that could be thrown. In the end, Benjamin Piercy brought the meeting to a reasonably dignified ending.

Davies and Savin had only made this ceremony possible by themselves putting up the Parliamentary Deposit; they had been appointed contractors to the company, but the partnership was on the slide, and soon after, the contract was given up. Of course, Whalley had a case. He claimed that if the contractors financed the construction and then leased the line, it reduced the Directors to being servants of the contractor. But 'he who pays the piper . . .'; being an MP and a gentleman did not entitle you to have your cake and eat it.

The new contractor was A.T. Gordon, and he completed fencing all the way to Newbridge by October 1861 and probably completed some of the engineering; the appointment of Overend & Watson as contractors in February 1862 was stated to be 'for the Brecon Extension', but really covered the whole line.

Amongst the problems which Piercy as Engineer had to face were 20 crossings of the Dulas, Marteg, Ithon and Wye rivers. For the wide multi-girder crossings a type of viaduct made up from tiers of standard cast-iron pillars with cross-bracing was used. Though cheap and quick, this method resulted in structures which limited engine weight in later years, even after most had been strengthened with encasing concrete. There was a good deal of rock cutting in the first few miles (construction started at the northern end) and a tunnel was required at Gilfach (Marteg) which was intended as a rock bore, but had to be brick-lined when the roof was found to be unstable. South of here the Wye Valley offered better conditions, but the railway could not follow the river through Rhayader, which town had to be passed high up to the west, with much embankment and a further short tunnel.

A number of engines must have been used on construction work, but only two are known. There is a photograph of a 0–4–0 named *Venus* working just south of Builth Wells; this is said to have been the engine of the same name from the Newcastle & Carlisle Railway, but this is not certain. A long-boiler 0−6−0 by Fossick & Hackworth is known to have been on the Mid-Wales contract in the south; this was sold in 1872 to the Carmarthen & Cardigan Railway and passed to the GWR, being scrapped at Swindon in 1889. It was named *Victor*.

Meanwhile a lot of activity had gone on south of Newbridge, but it was not railway-building. Various pressure groups had been formed as soon as the rumour of the sale of the Hay Tramroad became public. The biggest one was wedded to the continuance of the canal, and complained that the planned railway replacing the tramroad would be ¾ mile from the canal at its nearest point (not quite true) and well above the basin: 'all direct means of transporting heavy goods between the mineral districts and the best agricultural land in Brecknockshire, Radnorshire and Herefordshire would be destroyed'.

The route of the intended railway was disputed by others. Although it would follow mainly the course of the tramroad from Glasbury to Brecon, there were such tight curves on the actual tramroad that various pockets of land had to be bought to ease them. One of these was just east of Three Cocks, on the part that would become Mid-Wales Railway. In April 1859 the HH&B wrote politely to one Colonel Wood, an absentee landlord living at Chertsey, asking if he would accept shares in lieu of payment for a small parcel of land. He replied that if the railway 'were to make an attempt to run into my deer paddock, I will appeal to the House of Lords'. He did prepare an appeal, aided by Maybery, asking for the line to run from Glasbury church across the main road by Pipton House, and by the Old Forge over some meadows to Pontithel. This would have required at least one bridge, and the route east of the Afon Llynfi was in fact adhered to.

Because of this or some other complaint, John Cobb asked a local engineer, Mr Wylie, in April 1859 to inspect the track of the tramroad between Glasbury and Pontithel; Wylie confessed that he had already been over the route for the Shrewsbury & Hereford Railway 'to give evidence of its merits and deficiencies'.

Both the Mid-Wales contractors and Savin for the B&M were anxious to get on with construction between Three Cocks and Brecon, but were informed by their lawyers that they could not legally do so until the day after the final date for the purchase of the Hay Railway by the HH&B, which was 6th June, 1862; both railways therefore applied for and received Acts to allow their contractors into the property in June 1861. The Mid-Wales did not actually complete their purchase until 19th August, 1865; a week later the HH&B and B&M amalgamated, so no purchase was necessary there.

At Talyllyn Junction a triangular layout was adopted, and the Mid-Wales built a station at the North Junction (No. 1) with platforms for trains to Brecon and also to Dowlais, the latter being on the East Loop. The B&M built a station by the West Junction (No. 2). The ancient tunnel, opened in 1816, needed widening and track-lowering, a job which the Mid-Wales was no doubt glad to see done by the B&M.

The MWR published optimistic forecasts from time to time; in 1862 'it had made seventeen river and eight road diversions between Llanidloes and Rhayader, and three river viaducts had been completed'. The line 'would be open by the autumn of 1863'; but it was not, though the Brecon & Merthyr had their trains running from 1st May, 1863. The Mid-Wales managed a special train on 23rd August, 1864, and full goods services (apart from the east loop) by 1st September. The HH&B service from Hereford to Brecon was running by 19th September, and Mid-Wales passenger trains probably on 21st September, all these trains terminating at a station called Watton, built just above the canal basin on the outskirts of Brecon. It is not known for certain what locomotives were used; the historian C.R. Clinker has stated that Savin hired GWR engines for the Hereford trains until 1866. He had 27 engines (apart from contractors types) in 1864 for his various lines, but perhaps this was not enough. The MWR had no engines for a few months, but could have hired from Savin's sheds at Llanidloes and Brecon.

The days before opening had been rather fraught. At the B&M Board meeting on 26th August, 1864 Savin had announced 'the Brecon & Merthyr line at present ends in a field, but the Mid-Wales Railway is now open for goods traffic and will shortly be able to fulfil its undertaking to the Company'. This suggests that the east curve at Talyllyn must have been the last piece of construction, and Savin was referring to the ability to work their goods northwards from the junction, since his line from Brecon to Dowlais was already running. *Bradshaw's Manual* stated that the Mid-Wales would be open for passenger traffic from 1st September, but the *Brecon Journal* could only state on 17th September that 'it understood the Mid-Wales Railway would be open in a few days for passenger traffic'. The MWR pleaded non-delivery of carriages and in fact had no engines of its own; however it is known that special trains were run on 19th/20th September for Brecon Races, with borrowed engines.

The Mid-Wales had stations at Tylwch, Pantydwr, Rhayader, Doldowlod, Newbridge-on-Wye, Llechryd (later Builth Road), Builth Wells, Erwood, Boughrood, Three Cocks Junction (with the HH&B), Talgarth, Talyllyn Junction, and used the B&M station at Watton (Brecon). At Llanidloes it used the new joint station which the L&N had built to replace its original station. It caused quite a stir locally, the *Shrewsbury Chronicle* reporting on 25th April, 1862, 'The first stone of this fine structure intended for the purpose of the Llanidloes & Newtown, Manchester & Milford, and Mid-Wales Railway Companies, was laid on Thursday week . . . the event was followed by a supper to the workmen on the following day'.

Before ending this chapter, mention must be made of the amalgamation of the Llanidloes & Newtown, Oswestry & Newtown, Newtown & Machynlleth and Oswestry Ellesmere & Whitchurch into the Cambrian Railways in July 1864; the Aberystwyth & Welsh Coast (A&WCR) followed next year. The 1864 Amalgamation Bill preserved the Mid-Wales's rights concerning running powers; the 1865 Bill bringing in the A&WCR was actually opposed by the Mid-Wales, because of nervousness over running powers on the Coast Line, which it might have used if it had got through to Aberystwyth as intended. The Mid-Wales had acquired a formidable list of running powers, as had the other lines over it, but few were ever used, apart from the obvious ones such as that for the Mid-Wales over the B&M.

The 'joint line' from Llanidloes to Penpontbren was inspected by Captain Tyler in January 1864, and he was not satisfied with the gating of occupation crossings. His colleague Col Yolland went over it again in August, and passed it subject to 30 lb. chairs being used at rail joints and in the centres of each rail; he thought the 22 lb. ones used were not up to the 'heavy engines which the gradients on the Mid-Wales would require'. He was puzzled to find two lines running side by side all the way with no connection at the southern end; he would prefer a proper double junction, and up and down lines, and asked how it was proposed to work the line. The Resident Engineer informed him that the L&N was precluded from working the line in the Act under which it was built, and the Inspector asked plaintively to whom he should direct his enquiry; perhaps to the Mid-Wales and Brecon & Merthyr Railways whom he understood were to work the line; in any case it was 'a matter for their Lordships at the Board of Trade'. It seems unlikely that the B&M was planning any trains from Dowlais to Llanidloes via the Talyllyn east loop; no doubt Yolland misunderstood.

Three years later Colonel Yolland was back in the area attending a dinner given by Davies at Aberystwyth to celebrate the successful inspection of the Manchester & Milford's new main line via Trawscoed and the Ystwyth. As he listened to Davies explaining why he could never complete 'the old line over the mountains' (that is, via Llangurig) the Colonel would have understood why the junction he had inspected not so long ago at Penpontbren had an air of unreality.

Great Oak Street, Llanidloes

A turn of the century view of Great Oak Street, Llanidloes portraying the once, quiet peace before the motorcar!   *Oakwood Press*

Chapter Three
No Clear Signals

The Mid-Wales Railway was now open, being operated by the contractors, and locomotives and carriage stock were arriving; engine sheds were being built at Llanidloes, Builth Wells and Brecon, and a carriage workshop was to be set up at Builth. Traffic was coming from Dowlais over the Brecon & Merthyr Railway, but the connection to Merthyr, which would be more productive of through traffic, was not yet open. There were prospects in other quarters, however. The Manchester & Milford Railway had its line in place from Llanidloes to Llangurig; as with the MWR, the line down to Penpontbren belonged to the Llanidloes & Newtown. But no trains were running, for the company had changed its mind about the mile-long tunnel which would be needed south-west of Llangurig. It now intended to deviate from its approved route near Trawscoed, to cross the Tregaron Bog and run into Aberystwyth along the Ystwyth valley. The northern end of this new route was also that which the Mid-Wales aspired to in its planned branch from Rhayader; the M&M also had in mind a branch from its line down to Rhayader.

The spectacle of two impoverished companies fighting over some of the most barren parts of Mid-Wales cannot have pleased the shareholders, and it was as well that they decided to negotiate. In 1864 the two companies, joined by another not actually built, the Swansea & Aberystwyth, signed an Agreement which had Parliamentary force. The Mid-Wales would apply for powers to build a branch from Aber Marteg to Trawscoed, and from some point on this line to Llangurig to join up with the already-built portion of the M&M. The M&M would build its line from Ystrad Meurig, where it deviated from the original line to Llangurig, into Aberystwyth. It would also complete a triangle by a short spur from Ystrad Meurig to Yspytty Ystwyth on the MWR Trawscoed line. The M&M could thus run straight through to Llangurig, and the MWR would have running powers from Trawscoed to Aberystwyth.

Both companies obtained their Acts in 1865, and David Davies pushed hard to get his navvies to complete the M&M into Aberystwyth. The Mid-Wales for its part just sat on its hands. It may perhaps have looked more closely at the gradients on the lines it had agreed to. That from Aber Marteg would have used the upper part of the Wye Valley, and then followed the Nant-y-Dernol stream to a short tunnel and some cutting down to the Ystwyth valley. Gradients possibly as bad as 1 in 40 would have been needed. The Board was also rather pre-occupied in other directions; the Neath & Brecon Railway (N&B), which was approaching Brecon from the west, and might bring some traffic, now decided to go for a line from Devynock near Senny Bridge to Llangammarch Wells on the Central Wales Extension Railway. This would have meant that traffic instead of coming through Brecon and on to the Mid-Wales would in fact go straight on to the CWR. This scheme did not succeed, but was revived in 1882 and 1888 before being dropped.

Another company in that area was the Brecon & Llandovery Junction Railway; this the MWR backed, as it would apply for running powers from Brecon and thus get into Llandovery after all. But it was disappointed; the Brecon & Merthyr did a deal whereby it would allow the Neath & Brecon to make an end-on connection with it 20 chains west of the Watton station, if it would drop the Llandovery idea. This was agreed; the Mid-Wales had lost Llandovery yet again.

Meanwhile, the MWR was doing its best to serve Brecon; in July 1865 through coaches to Aberystwyth were inaugurated. Next month a through carriage from Hereford to the resort was added; this took just over five hours, which was not bad considering it had to be attached and detached three times.

In 1866 something happened that David Davies had seen coming, but was totally unexpected by most people; Savin went bankrupt in February of that year. As often happens, he fell from the top rung of the ladder; he had nearly completed building the Coast Line, had many other irons in the fire, and stood well with the newly-amalgamated Cambrian Railways. It was rumoured that the Mid-Wales might join the mighty Savin empire, for it was the only link needed to give Savin a continuous run of 'his' railways from Whitchurch to Newport. The Brecon & Merthyr and HH&B were now forced to take over the operating of their own railways, and soon the side effects of the crash also caused the Mid-Wales contractors to withdraw from their operating agreement. The Mid-Wales was fortunate in one respect; it knew where its locomotives were. The railways in the Savin empire found out, when the Receiver got busy, that many engines on one company's books were 'on loan' to another; the Mid-Wales must have been witness to the shame-faced return from the Brecon & Merthyr of some locomotives which in fact were owned by the Cambrian.

Another event a few months later, the collapse of the Overend & Gurney bank, also dampened local optimism and may have been the trigger which caused the Mid-Wales to hire out four of its engines and some carriages and goods wagons; these were later sold. Certainly 12 engines seemed too much for a line operating three trains per day plus some goods traffic, though had any of the proposed branch lines come to pass they would no doubt have been needed. Nevertheless, the MWR had by no means retired into its shell. It acquired running powers to Hereford, and over the Brecon & Merthyr's new branch line to Merthyr, hoping thereby to obtain the same facilities over the Vale of Neath Railway; it also made 'arrangements' with various small railways which it hoped at some time to reach.

Until 1866 the Mid-Wales and the Brecon & Merthyr had been worked by their contractors (who were not the same) and there seems to have been no formal agreements on rates. In that year however the two companies agreed to disagree and to ask the Board of Trade to appoint an arbitrator. The subsequent Agreement is a document in archaic style beginning with salutations from Mark Huish, the arbitrator 'To all to whom these presents shall come I Mark Huish of Bonchurch in the Isle of Wight [he had retired there after leaving the LNWR] send greeting . . .' The Acts under which the railways were set up are recited; the draughtsman seems to have been put out by the number of the Mid-Wales Company's Acts and after reciting six of them inserted 'other Acts in the Counties of Montgomery, Radnor and Brecon'. First of all, it grants the B&M the right to run over any part of the Mid-Wales, and vice versa. It then directs that the traffic of both companies in Brecon Station shall be managed and worked exclusively by the Brecon Company; likewise bookings, parcels, goods, cattle etc. However if they wished the Mid-Wales could have an office in the station, and keep a man there 'to watch over their interests'.

The overhead costs of the station would be divided between the Companies in proportion to the number of trains run in and out by each; either company requiring night staff would pay them itself. If the Mid-Wales required any sheds for locomotive or other purposes, the B&M must allot the land, but the Mid-Wales would pay the cost. Water would be supplied at cost.

The same agreement covered the use of the lines and stations at Talyllyn; these were 'being erected partly on the land of both Companies, and as no evidence had been given of proprietorship, each shall have the use of them as before.' No charge would be made for using the sidings. The Mid-Wales should pay for the No. 1 signal box and signalman (that is the north one) while the B&M should pay for No. 2 (west) and No. 3 (east). After stating that the principles of working expenses at Brecon should be '*mutatis mutandis*' the Arbitrator stated that the same principles should apply at Talgarth and Three Cocks, no rent at either station being chargeable to the Brecon Company. It seems from this that the 'amalgamation' between the B&M and HH&B was at that time accepted, and that trains to Hereford were regarded as included in the B&M side of the Agreement.

The tolls to be paid by each company to the other for use of their lines was to be 1¾d. per mile for first class, 1¼d. second and three farthings third. However day tickets were 2¼d., 1¾d. and 1d. return. Rates for goods traffic were also fixed, and it was directed that the 29 chains of Mid-Wales railway extending from Three Cocks towards Hereford should be taken as half a mile in calculating tolls. (Huish actually gave this as '38 chains or thereabouts'.) The reason why the MWR owned this short stretch was that the intention had been to make a triangular junction here, as at Talyllyn; there would have been an East Junction where the line entered the cutting to go under the Glasbury road.

The parties were not totally satisfied with the arbitration, and Capt. Huish agreed to answer some questions put to him in writing; these appear over the signature of A. Henshaw for the B&M and H. Broughton for the Mid-Wales. The first question, relating to credits for carting at Brecon, is too complex to quote. The second, as to what the charge should be for dogs, received the succinct reply 'The tolls on dogs to be as on parcels'. The fourth question was also easy to answer: 'hides' was a clerical error for 'tiles'. The third and fifth questions dealt with classifications of goods and minerals; it seems the forms supplied by the Railway Clearing House did not classify items in the same way that the Award did, nor did the original Acts of the two companies agree on classification. Capt. Huish ruled that this should be as contained in the Mid-Wales 1859 Act; as both parties had agreed to abide by his ruling, this was the end of the matter.

The Agreement did not remain in force for long. On 3rd June, 1867 the Neath & Brecon Railway opened a new station in the town, leading to changes. Brecon had three passenger stations, and their history from 1864 until 1874, by which time there was only one, is somewhat complex. The Brecon & Merthyr first built the station called Watton, just above the Watton canal basin, on the east side of the town. Here there were goods sidings also, and engine sheds — a 'Savin' shed for locomotives working the B&M and HH&B and later a separate one for the Mid-Wales. The Mid-Wales did not have to pay any rent for this, but had to pay 9d. to the B&M every time an engine was turned on the table. The station was probably a fairly rough one; for the next century a single platform with wooden buildings remained there.

Soon after opening, the B&M built a branch line of 55 chains, at a higher level than Watton, from a junction east of that station called Heol Lladron Junction; this was to meet up with the Neath & Brecon Railway approaching from the east. There was a spur line running down to the east end of the Watton sidings, presumably to enable N&B engines to reach the sheds, but owing to disputes between the companies, according to a Board of Trade report, the B&M would not allow the N&B to use it; the latter set up its own goods station later at Ely Place.

By 1868 Watton was somewhat crowded, with trains of the Mid-Wales, B&M and HH&B (worked by the other two) using it, and the Mid-Wales decided to throw in with the Neath & Brecon at their new station at Mount Street, even putting an Act through Parliament permitting them to have a joint station. In the event, however, the Brecon & Merthyr built a fine new station at Free Street on the line from Heol Lladron to the junction with the N&B. This was opened on 1st March, 1871, and in May the Mid-Wales decided to use it also. The Neath & Brecon trains, now being worked by the Midland Railway, stayed with Mount Street until 1874 when they also joined the party, much to the relief of passengers who had never been sure which station to use. According to Mr D.S.M. Barrie, passengers off the Neath & Brecon for Watton were sometimes placed on an engine and run down to a point on the high level line above Watton station, since the B&M would not allow the N&B to use the spur line down to it.

Under the 1871 Agreement the Mid-Wales paid the B&M £400 per annum plus £400 for working expenses for both the Brecon and Talyllyn stations. The B&M built a new station at the latter place which opened on 1st October, 1869; it was right up against the east tunnel mouth; while it was being built its old station, called Brynderwen, could not be used, so trains to Dowlais set back from the east junction to the platform of the Mid-Wales station on the east loop. The official date at which the MWR gave up its Talyllyn station at the north junction is 15th May, 1878; however it is likely that its trains earlier stopped at both stations for connecting purposes, or possibly it was only kept open for the through trains via the east loop.

The stations at Talyllyn have always been something of a puzzle; the timetables never admitted to there being more than one station at Talyllyn so they are no help in deciding how it all worked. It seems likely that the Mid-Wales was more interested in South Wales than in Brecon, and to have a platform on the through line, their station had to be sited on the inside 'V' at the north junction. The Brynderwen station built by the B&M, if it was to serve itself and the HH&B, must be sited between the west junction and the mouth of the tunnel. It must be emphasised that Talyllyn was purely an interchange point; there was nothing there to stop for; in 1900 Brynderwen had nine houses and Talyllyn eleven. So how did they manage with two stations 600 yards apart? One thing seems certain; in the case of the best morning train to Dowlais and Merthyr from Llanidloes in 1869, which was allowed only five minutes at Talyllyn, the passengers must have been set down on the north loop platform of the Mid-Wales station, to find the Brecon & Merthyr train to Dowlais waiting in the east loop platform; unless of course the Mid-Wales train stopped in Brynderwen, though there is no certainty that there was a passing loop there. The equivalent north-bound train was shown as arriving and departing at the same time at Talyllyn, suggesting an actual through train.

Another puzzling feature is that the Brecon & Merthyr locomotive shed, built it is believed in 1869, was connected to the Mid-Wales-owned part of the east loop, and it was not until some 20 years later that a spur was built across to it from the B&M-owned west loop. Of course the B&M had running powers over the Mid-Wales, and could use the north junction to reach the shed; it may have been placed in that position as being more convenient for exchanging engines on south-to-north trains, passenger and goods.

Little is known of the B&M Brynderwen station; it is assumed to have been on the Brecon side of the west junction, for the reason given above; but if so it must have had short platforms, as surprise was expressed over the 1871 station that the platforms ran right up to the tunnel mouth. This was considered dangerous as the driver of a train would arrive from darkness and would not see anything standing in the platform until the last few seconds. Special warning lights were set up in the tunnel.

The Mid-Wales seems to have enjoyed a close relationship with the London & North Western Railway at this time. An 1869 timetable bill which has survived shows that all trains in both directions made a five minute (or near) connection at Builth Road to through carriages to LNWR stations in London, the Midlands and the North. Connections to and from South Wales at Talyllyn were not so good; however they were better between the MWR and Neath & Brecon at Brecon, confirming that the Mid-Wales was using the NBR station at Mount Street. The bill makes no mention whatever of the Cambrian Railway and shows trains only as far as Builth Road (it does not use the proper name Llechryd for the low level station). It recognises the Midland Railway only insofar as it gives one down arrival time at Glasbury. It promises that passengers only have to change carriages once (presumably at Builth Road) and if true means that in 1869 one could travel from Brecon to Edinburgh in 13 hours only changing once!

As stated above, the Hereford Hay & Brecon had been running its own trains since the Savin crash. It had little experience, as, when partially open

MID-WALES RAILWAY

TIME TABLE for OCTOBER, 1869,

SHEWING THE

DIRECT ROUTE

To and from London, Manchester, Liverpool, Birmingham, Stafford-shire, &c., &c., by the London and North Western Railway.

IMPORTANT NOTICE.

Passengers can obtain Through Tickets between the following Stations at the Fares quoted by this Route and only have to change Carriages once during the Journey.

UP TRAINS.

	WEEK DAYS.				
	a.m.	a.m.	a.m.	a.m.	p.m.
Leave NEATH	...	...	8 35	11 10	3 15
" DEFYNNOCK	...	...	9 35	12 20	4 25
Arrive BRECON	...	...	10 0	12 45	4 50
Leave NEWPORT	7 35	10 45	...	...	...
" MACHEN	8 0	11 12	...	...	...
" PENGAM	8 26	11 15	...	...	...
" RHYMNEY	8 5	11 13	...	...	...
" DOWLAIS TOP	9 10	12 13	...	...	...
" DANT	9 17	12 20	...	...	...
" DOWLAIS	9 5	12 5	...	...	...
" MERTHYR	8 35	12 0	...	...	...
" CEFN	10 10	1 2	...	...	...
" TALYBONT	10 20	1 20	...	...	...
Arrive TALYLLYN					

	a.m.	a.m.	a.m.	p.m.	p.m.
Leave Brecon	7 45	10 50	2 0	6 30	...
" Talyllyn	...	11 0	...	6 40	...
" Talgarth	8 5	11 12	2 20	6 53	...
" Hay	...	...	...	...	...
" Glasbury	8 13	11 20	2 30	7 0	...
" Three Cocks	...	11 28	2 38	7 8	...
" Boughrood	...	11 ...	...	...	...

DOWN TRAINS.

	WEEK DAYS.				
	p.m.	a.m.	a.m.	a.m.	noon.
Leave LONDON Broad Street	9 15	...	8 25	...	11 25
" (Euston)	8 40	...	9 0	...	12 0
" BIRMINGHAM	10 30	8 0	11 30	...	12 30
" STAFFORD	2 13	9 5	12 35	...	3 30
" EDINBURGH	4 15	9 30	...	...	3 45
" GLASGOW	4 0	9 10	...	...	...
" CARLISLE	7 50	12 47	...	8 45	...
" PRESTON	11 14	3 42	9 30	11 44	12 10
" LIVERPOOL	11 15	7 20	10 15	11 30	12 50
" LEEDS	9 45	...	9 55	9 10	12 40
" HUDDERSFIELD	11 7	...	10 50	9 45	1 20
" MANCHESTER	10 55	7 30	1 50	11 40	1 30
" HOLYHEAD	8 15	1 50	...	8 30	9 15
" BIRKENHEAD	10 15	6 53	7 25	11 40	1 15
" CHESTER	11 0	7 25	8 20	12 10	1 15
" CREWE	8 6	7 35	...	12 30	1 15
" SHREWSBURY	7 0	10 10	1 50	2 20	5 40
" CRAVEN ARMS	8 5	11 5	2 53	...	6 0
" LLANDRINDOD WELLS	9 28	12 38	4 3	...	8 25
Arrive BUILTH ROAD	9 41	12 50	4 18	...	8 40

BRECON. THREE COCKS. TALGARTH. BUILTH.

Departures from Builth (top table)

Leave	a.m.	a.m.	p.m.	p.m.	p.m.
Leave Builth Road	9 45	12 55	4 25		8 45
" Builth	9 50	1 0	4 30		8 50
" Aberedw					
" Erwood	10 ...	1 15	4 50		9 12
" Boughrood	10 23	1 25	4 56		9 18
" Three Cocks	10 30	1 33	5 3		
" Glasbury					
" Hay	10 40	1 40			9 25
" Talgarth	11 0		5 15		
" Talyllyn	11 10	2 0	5 30		9 45
Arrive Brecon					

Leave TALYLLYN	1 15				
" TALYBONT	2 15				
" CEFN	2 25				
" MERTHYR	2 20				
" DOWLAIS	2 20				
" PANT	2 12				
" DOWLAIS TOP	2 18				
" RHYMNEY					
" PENGAM	2 45				
" MACHEN	3 20				
Arrive NEWPORT	3 50			5 45	
Leave BRECON	11 55			6 9	
" DEFYNOCK	12 20			7 20	
Arrive NEATH	1 31				

LONDON and connections (centre table)

(columns: 1st Class, 2nd Class, Gov. — Brecon / Three Cocks / Talgarth)

	1st Class d.	2nd Class d.	Gov. d.
LONDON (Euston)			
Birmingham (New-st.)			
Stafford			
Shrewsbury			
Crewe			
Manchester			
Liverpool			
Chester			
Leeds			
Preston			
Huddersfield			

All Trains on the Mid-Wales Line are First, Second, and Third Class.

ASK FOR TICKETS BY LONDON and NORTH WESTERN and MID-WALES ROUTE.

Down table (bottom left)

Leave BUILTH ROAD	8 55	12	1	3	8	7 46
Arrive LLANDRINDOD WELLS	9 11	12 16	3 24	8	8	8 1
" CRAVEN ARMS	10 30	1 32	4 42	9	9 23	
" SHREWSBURY	11 23	2 20	5 20	10	0	
" CREWE	12 43	3 50	6 51	10	0	
" CHESTER	2 26	4 40	7 58	2	18	
" BIRKENHEAD	3 30	5 27	9	0	3 5	
" HOLYHEAD	7 0	8 15	12 50	4 45		
" MANCHESTER	2 0	5 10	7 45	2 45		
" HUDDERSFIELD	2 52	6 25	9 48			
" LEEDS	3 35	7 10	11 10			
" LIVERPOOL	2 30	5 40	8 0	4 0		
" PRESTON	2 35	5 55	9 0	4 0		
" CARLISLE	5 45	9 15		4 0		
" GLASGOW	9 30	12 40		7 10		
" EDINBURGH	9 10	12 30		7 10		
" STAFFORD	1 35	4 0	6 45	11 7		
" BIRMINGHAM	3 0	5 25	7 50	2 30		
" LONDON, (Euston)	5 15	9 15	10 30	3 15		
" " Broad Street	5 40	9 40				

NOTICES.

This Company will not undertake the conveyance of Cattle by Passenger Trains.

Passengers, to ensure being booked should be at the Stations Five Minutes before the Time fixed for the Departure of the Trains. The times shewn on this Bill are the times at which the Trains are intended to arrive at and depart from the several Stations; the Company will adopt every means to insure punctuality, but cannot guarantee the times being kept under all circumstances, nor will they be responsible for delay. The Station Clocks are set to Greenwich Time, and are faster by eleven minutes than the true time of the district.

Granting Tickets to Passengers to places off the Company's Line is an arrangement made for the greater convenience of the Public, but the Company do not hold themselves responsible for any delay, loss, or injury whatsoever, arising of their Line, or from the acts or defaults of other parties, or for the correctness of the times over other Lines, or for the arrival of this Company's Trains in time for the nominally corresponding Train of any other Company. When their Trains do not arrive in time, such Tickets will be available onward by the first practicable Train, and the Tickets are issued subject to this understanding—Passengers are booked at the intermediate Stations conditionally upon their being room in the Trains.—Large parties wishing to travel by any particular Train should give notice, so that extra carriages may be attached at the Terminal Stations.

Market Tickets are issued to Brecon, Builth and Talgarth on Market and Fair Days.

Notice—MARKET TICKETS.—It is particularly requested that Passengers will take notice that Market Tickets are intended for the convenience of Passengers attending markets, and will be forfeited if used to any Station beyond that to which issued.

Return Tickets.—The Scale of Periods for Return Tickets being available is as follows:—To all Stations within a distance of 30 miles inclusive, one day; 125 miles inclusive, two days; 200 miles inclusive, three days; 300 miles inclusive, four days.

Children's Tickets.—Children under Three Years of Age are conveyed free; above Three and under Twelve at half-fares.

Llandrindod Wells.—Cheap Tickets are issued from all Stations on Saturdays to these Wells.

Passengers' Luggage.—Each First Class Passenger is allowed 120lbs.; each Second Class Passenger, 100lbs. weight of Luggage free of charge—the same not being merchandise or other articles carried for hire or profit; any excess above those weights will be charged. For the protection of their Luggage, Passengers are recommended to have their names and destination clearly stated upon, and properly fastened to each article. The Company will not be responsible for articles left in any of their Offices for the convenience of the Owners, unless deposited in the Booking Office, and the fixed charge of Twopence per package paid.

(N) A Mail Omnibus runs between Llandovery and Defynock, meeting the 8.10 a.m. Train from Brecon, and the 3.15 p.m. train from Neath.

General Manager's Office, Brecon, September, 1869.

PRINTED AT THE "BRECON COUNTY TIMES," STEAM PRINTING WORKS, BRECON.

F. BROUGHTON, General Manager.

This poster was issued by the Mid-Wales Railway to advertise itself as the route for travel from South Wales to the North of England, although it only brought in revenue from the line between Talyllyn and Builth Road. It is remarkable in showing Neath & Brecon Railway and Brecon & Merthyr Railway stations; note that morning passengers from various places having arrived at Builth Road at 11.55 am had only to wait six minutes to be whisked onwards to the Midlands, Scotland or London.

Author's Collection

in 1862 and 1863, it had been operated by the West Midland Railway (WMR), and, for a few months, by the GWR after it absorbed the WMR. From 1865 the HH&B was amalgamated with the B&M, though it turned out that this was not legally done, and three years later the two were 'dis-amalgamated'. Some engines had been ordered by Savin for the HH&B but these had disappeared into his stock list, and for a time trains from Brecon to Hereford were worked by both the Mid-Wales and B&M. The timetables showed 'B&M' or 'MW' at the top of the column, necessarily since they ran into different stations at Hereford, the HH&B using its own Moorfields terminus, and the MWR the more convenient GWR Barton station, although the Act giving it the powers to do so was not passed until 1872 after it ceased to work there.

From 1st October, 1868 the Mid-Wales took over the working on its own; it would perhaps have been a good idea to make this permanent, and the offer was made by the HH&B, but the MWR dithered and in the meantime a powerful outside company had decided to intervene: the Midland Railway. The reason for the Mid-Wales's reluctance might have been the complexity of the mess left by Savin. The Brecon & Merthyr annual report for 1870, issued on 28th February, 1871, stated that the HH&B 'Disamalgamation Account' had just been closed by a payment by the B&M of some £7,000, but, turning to the other matter, 'it has proved impossible to obtain the attention of Mr Savin's inspectors'.

The Midland had been planning to reach South Wales for many years, but was always frustrated by the GWR. The plan now was to lease at least two railways, the HH&B and Swansea Vale, and to join them up by running powers over the Neath & Brecon Railway and a junction line with the Swansea Vale, to be provided between Colbren Junction and Ynys-y-Geinon Junction by yet another railway, the Swansea Vale & Brecon Junction. The Midland duly took over the working from Hereford to Three Cocks on 1st October, 1869, and leased the Swansea Vale on 1st July, 1874, having got the junction line from Colbren open by 10th November, 1873. But there were hiccups; the Great Western challenged the inheritance by the MR of running powers from Hereford to Worcester; moreover the Mid-Wales informed it that any running powers they thought they had between Three Cocks and Talyllyn, inherited from the HH&B, were accorded on a friendly basis only. Worse, the GWR utterly refused to allow the Midland to use a link between the HH&B terminus at Moorfields in Hereford and the main station, and blocked it with rolling stock. Finally, with an injunction from the Lords of Appeal, the MR got this unblocked, and the way was open in 1878 for a service from Birmingham to Swansea via a number of railways including the Mid-Wales.

The Midland had originally worked complete trains from Worcester to Hereford but gave these up in favour of through carriages on Great Western trains. An MR engine worked these from the GWR main station to Barton station, and then reversed into Moorfields, the terminus for Brecon. To tidy things up, the MR bought the HH&B outright in 1886, and in 1893 spurs were built from Barton Junction in Hereford to Moorfields and from Barton Junction to Brecon Curve Junction, allowing through coaches from Swansea via Brecon and Three Cocks to run direct to Barrs Court station, Hereford. The Midland had taken over the working of the Neath & Brecon line from Brecon to Ynys-y-Geinon Junction in 1874. To bring the story right up to date, the through coaches from Swansea to Birmingham ran until 1916 and to Hereford until 1931 — an important part of the revenue of the Mid-Wales line.

It will be recalled that the Mid-Wales had obtained Acts in 1865 for its branches in the Trawscoed area, but had done nothing in the way of construction. On 23rd April, 1872 an article in the *Newtown & Welshpool Express* stated 'there is a probability of the line which for years has been idle between Penpontbren Junction and Llangurig being brought into use. We are informed that orders have been given for the erection of a junction at the former place'. This may seem confusing; a clue lies in the fact that the Manchester & Milford Railway claimed that the arrangement for paying their share of the joint station at Llanidloes (that is, joint between the Cambrian, Mid-Wales, and M&M) did not come into force until 'a junction at Penpontbren is open'. They now claimed that this junction was not open, and their debt to the Cambrian for station and junction costs was invalid. The Cambrian must therefore have done something at this time to counter this claim; whether the signal box and signals were built with the line in 1860 is not certain. Perhaps the Cambrian had only to send a man to occupy the box; it was only a few weeks after the press comment above that the junction was pronounced officially open. As far as is known, the M&M never paid their debt, and they never used the junction.

The Mid-Wales had to go to Parliament in 1869 and again in 1872 to obtain extensions of time on their Western Extensions Act; the Manchester & Milford attempted without success to build into these extension Acts a heavy penalty for any further delay. The next thing that happened was traumatic for the M&M; the Mid-Wales applied to Parliament in 1876 to abandon its Llangurig and Aberystwyth branches. One can understand the chagrin shown; under the 1864 agreement the Manchester & Milford had got away with obtaining a through route via Llanidloes to the north of England by agreeing to build only the short line between Ystrad Meurig and Yspytty Ystwyth; now the whole thing was threatened with collapse. They applied to the Law, but the Solicitor-General handed down the opinion that the Mid-Wales had only agreed to apply for the Acts; it had not agreed to build the lines. So the aggrieved party raised a Bill for compensation for loss of traffic and for the Llanidloes costs (which they had not paid in fact). The tearful Directors claimed that the Mid-Wales branches would have been their life-line. However, the Mid-Wales's view that the Bill was 'unreasonable, vexatious, and vindictive' was sustained in the Lords, and it was thrown out. This was not the last attempt to build a railway across the area south of the Cambrian Mountains, but it was a convenient ending for the Mid-Wales; the sorry story is still witnessed today by the bare embankment from Penpontbren to Llangurig and half-a-mile beyond.

Meanwhile in July 1872 the line had enjoyed a highly profitable day when David Davies gave an enormous party for his son's coming-of-age in a field by Llandinam station. Four train-loads of officials and miners from his

Ocean Collieries in South Wales were brought up. A photograph of the crowded sidings shows Cambrian Railway coaches, so empty stock must have run down and back again after the event — something to justify the many passing loops the railway was blessed with.

It is a fact that the long eastern border of Cardiganshire has never had a railway crossing it. The various attempts to do so in the north have already been described; now there was to be an attempt from the south. There was already a railway at Kington, close to the Radnorshire border, connecting through Leominster to Worcester. There had also been for many decades a plateway from Kington down to Eardisley, connecting with the Hay Tramroad. Savin set about converting this to a real railway, and at the same time several other projects were mooted; the Mid-Wales wished to build from Rhayader to Penybont on the Central Wales Railway, and other parties planned to build an extension westwards from Kington through New Radnor and Penybont to Rhayader. The Mid-Wales Bill had failed in 1865; it was some years later, in 1872, that the extension from Kington was raised again, as the Worcester & Aberystwyth Railway. The original extension had actually got across the Welsh border but stopped at New Radnor, only seven miles from Penybont.

Old Swan, Rhayader.

A turn of the century view of the crossroads at the then quiet town of Rhayader.
Courtesy Mrs Powell

A few letters remaining in the archives of the Harpton Estate cast some light on this affair, and indicates why it failed. Mr R.D.G. Price was entrusted with the job of whipping up support, and complained bitterly of lack of interest, especially in the Penybont area. The Rev. Sir Gilbert Lewis of Harpton Court did come up with £1,000, but shrewdly stipulated that he would only contribute further if his debentures in the Eardisley & Kington Railway were redeemed at par. The line was to take the previous route, running to Rhayader after crossing the Central Wales at Penybont; however, in an effort to reduce the sum needed to be raised, the company decided to alter the route to join the Mid-Wales Railway at Llanelwedd near Builth. Mr Price wrote again to Sir Gilbert, but got a dusty answer. 'It is a matter of indifference to myself whether the line goes to Rhayader or Builth; I have had enough of railway-making and will decline again to take shares'.

The company decided, in spite of this rebuff, to spend some money on dropping the Rhayader Bill in 1876 and raising a new one for Builth. However there was still general apathy, and it failed. It is worth noting that the same scheme was raised again in 1898 as the East & West Wales Railway. This used the Rhayader route, and intended running up the Wye Valley parallel with the Mid-Wales line to Aber Marteg, then continuing up the valley on the route of the much earlier Mid-Wales Llangurig branch to that place, and tunnelling through the mountains to reach Trawscoed, to run into Aberystwyth over the Manchester & Milford Railway. Thus this proposal embodied many of the worst points of the various schemes which had gone before; Parliament thought it would be too costly and threw it out.

A LIST OF THE MAIN MID-WALES RAILWAY ACTS

(indicating each one's primary purposes; they of course also included other clauses)

22–3	V.c.lxiii	1859	Making the line from Llanidloes to Newbridge
23–4	V.c.cxxxiii	1860	Deviations and financial
24–5	V.c.lxv	1861	Extension to join the Hay Tramroad, and to purchase part
25–6	V.c.clvi	1862	Arrangement for Llanidloes Joint Line
26–7	V.c.ii	1863	Financial
26–7	V.c.lxxx	1863	Powers to run over Brecon & Merthyr Railway: to construct Llangurig Branch
27–8	V.c.cxlii	1864	Powers for junction line with Central Wales Railway
29–30	V.c.cx	1865	Financial
28–9	V.c.clix	1865	Powers for Eastern Extensions
28–9	V.c.ccclxxi	1865	Powers for Western Extensions; abandon Llangurig Branch
32–3	V.c.cxiii	1869	To abandon CWR link line and Eastern Extensions; to use NBR Mount Street station, Brecon
35–6	V.c.xlvii	1872	Running powers over part of GWR to Barton station, Hereford

MID-WALES RAILWAY.

THE ANNUAL ARRANGEMENTS FOR THE ISSUE OF

TOURIST TICKETS

(AVAILABLE FOR TWO MONTHS FROM DATE OF ISSUE)

At Stations on the BRECON and MERTHYR, the CAMBRIAN, the LONDON and NORTH WESTERN, GREAT WESTERN, MIDLAND, MANCHESTER, SHEFFIELD, and LINCOLNSHIRE, and other Railways, to Stations on the

MID-WALES RAILWAY,

AND ALSO

TICKETS OF CIRCULAR TOURS

EMBRACING

THE MID-WALES RAILWAY,

Are now in operation for the SUMMER MONTHS; and the Public are invited to visit the Magnificent Scenery of the upper portion of the RIVER WYE, which is unequalled in Wales, and through which passes

THE MID-WALES RAILWAY

☞ *The Line extends through a Panorama of grand MOUNTAIN and RIVER SCENERY; and good SALMON, TROUT, and other FISHING can be obtained near most of the Stations on the Line. Within easy walking distance of*

BUILTH STATION

ARE SITUATE

FAMOUS MINERAL SPRINGS OF SALINE, SULPHUR, AND CHALYBEATE WATERS,

Equal to those of Harrogate, and possessing great health-restoring power; while

MID-WALES RAILWAY—Continued.

A writer in the *Saturday Review* says: "Nowhere else are there River Systems to be found of the magnitude and incessant scenic variety of those in South Wales; nor anywhere in the Districts we have mentioned (Westmoreland, &c.) are the hills so bold, so finely formed, so precipitous, as here. Indeed the Brecknockshire Beacons will stand a comparison with most of the summits of North Wales." The Hon. F. GREVILLE in writing of

RHAYADER

about 14 miles north of Builth says: "I am well aware of the difficulty men have in deciding where to go, and with a fair prospect of sport; here is a place I can confidently recommend you to, and with equal assurance any number of your friends."

Special Fares are arranged between Stations on the

Mid-Wales Railway

And LLANDRINDOD WELLS, ABERYSTWITH, DOLGELLEY, BARMOUTH, and adjoining Lines.

TO PIC-NIC AND PLEASURE PARTIES.

RETURN TICKETS of all classes are issued, at about a FARE and QUARTER each, between Stations on the MID-WALES RAILWAY; and, by arrangement with the Companies, the same facilities are extended from MID-WALES STATIONS to Station on the Brecon and Merthyr, Neath and Brecon, and Midland (Hereford, Hay, and Brecon and Swansea Sections) Railways, and *vice versa.*

THE OTTER HOUNDS OF MAJOR THE HONOURABLE GEOFFREY HILL HUNT THE RIVER WYE.

During the Summer, grand Sport being generally obtained. Head-Quarters,

BUILTH.

In fact the lovely Scenery and manifold attractions of the MID-WALES RAILWAY ought to decide for thousands that difficult question asked yearly—"WHERE SHALL WE GO?"

Programmes of Times, Fares, &c., with descriptions of the different places, names of Hotels, &c., will be sent upon application to

FRANK GRUNDY,

GENERAL MANAGER.

Address BRECON.

Chapter Four

The Independent Years

The company had by no means cleared its debts before opening, and it appears that the traffic coming in for the first few years did not create much optimism amongst those who were owed money. In 1869 a group of them became sufficiently nervous to insist on the ownership of all the locomotives and rolling stock being vested in two of their number, Abel Chapman and John Borradaile. Four years later little had happened, so this consortium took the Mid-Wales Railway to Court to pursue their claim. No doubt they felt in a strong position, being in charge of the things that enabled it to run. The Directors did surprisingly well, perhaps because of a strong counter-attack. They stated that although they had the use of all the assigned engines and vehicles, they were still not enough to run the railway; the creditors' petition was thrown out, and the Directors were given permission to raise a further £20,000 in debentures, partly to satisfy accrued interest, but also to purchase further locomotives.

It is not clear why eight engines were not enough to run the rather sparse service; however the company did duly spend some of the money on two new 0–6–0 engines from Sharp, Stewart. All the original ones had come from Kitsons, but the neighbouring railways run by Savin were equipped with Sharp, Stewart engines, the Cambrian having found the particular class selected to be very satisfactory.

The fact that the company finances were in a sorry state was partly due to the cost of so many applications to Parliament for branch lines which were not built; there was the London office to be paid for, and other standing charges such as those paid to the Cambrian for the joint line and Llanidloes station, and to the Brecon & Merthyr for the joint Brecon stations. On the credit side, some coal was passing through, as well as passenger traffic from the Welsh Valleys, timber traffic, lime and various sundries such as dead rabbits; there was the regular income from the Midland Railway too.

The original agreement with the Midland, a Lease Act of 1874, taking in much of the first HH&B agreement of 1869, expired on 31st December, 1876. Now the two companies could not reach agreement on rates, and it was not until February 1878 that they were able to do so. Basically, the Midland was to retain 20 per cent of tolls over the Three Cocks to Talyllyn section for passenger traffic, and 25 per cent for goods. The tolls the Midland were to pay included:

General goods	2¼d. per ton	Passengers 1st single	1½d. per mile
Minerals	1d.	2nd	1d. „ „
Granite & Lime	1d.	3rd	¾d. „ „
Coal and coke	⅝d.	Parcels	1d.
Cattle and horses	1d. per head	Fish	2d. per ton mile
Calves and pigs	½d. per head	Horse by passenger train	2d. per head per mile
		Carriage	3d. „
		Carriage (Railway)	4d.
		Dog	1d.
		Corpse	4½d.

It is interesting that the most expensive passenger was a corpse: on some railways this was quite a large traffic at that time; a few carriages had corpse compartments but it is not known that the Mid-Wales had any such. The reference to passengers by private railway carriage presumably meant 'privately hired'; the only actual private carriage known in the area was that of Earl Vane, and this was at the time being used at his seat in Northumberland.

In 1879 the debenture-holders went to Court in the Chancery Division, and a Receiver was appointed. It appeared that the company had issued £275,706 in debentures and was unable to meet the interest. The proceedings were long and dull, but in the end the action was dismissed and the Receiver discharged. The company was allowed to raise a further £40,000 in debentures, and a Scheme of Arrangement was drawn up under which holders of 'A' stock would receive 4 per cent from 1st July, 1879 and of 'B' stock 3½ per cent. Most of the new capital would of course be consumed in paying back interest to existing debenture-holders; it was a delaying operation, and it did not solve anything.

One thing that worked to the advantage of the Mid-Wales was the growing popularity of Aberystwyth as a holiday resort. Though its direct line had failed, it could feed visitors to Aberystwyth via Moat Lane Junction. Now that the Manchester & Milford worked only to Pencader there was not much competition from there, and the LNWR line from Swansea and Carmarthen via Shrewsbury and Welshpool was very roundabout. Savin had a stake in Aberystwyth, and he tried to develop two more nearby resorts, Ynyslas and Borth. The former failed, due to the marshy ground, but the latter became a fairly popular place, and Savin's great Grand Hotel built near Borth station sat in majesty until a few years ago. Though the Cambrian was the main gainer, these places were very popular with people from the Welsh Valleys and a good deal of mileage over the Mid-Wales resulted.

From 1874 there had been a thrice-weekly service from Neath to Llanid-loes with through coaches to Aberystwyth; Mid-Wales engines worked through to Neath. From 1880 the Mid-Wales provided through carriages from Cardiff (Rhymney Railway) to run via Bargoed and Talyllyn Junction to Aberystwyth. By 1884 these had become a regular summer service from Cardiff (Queen Street) and Newport (High Street), which picked up coaches from Merthyr at Pontsticill Junction (B&M) and after running through the Talyllyn east loop, picked up more coaches from Hereford at Three Cocks Junction.

At about this time the connection at Builth Road with the Central Wales was altered to take passenger traffic, but does not seem to have done so at that time. From the tourism point of view, its only value would have been to put Builth Wells on a direct service with the other 'Wells', Llandrindod, Llanwrtyd and Llangamarch, but this would have required a double reverse at Builth Road and no doubt what was in fact done, having shuttle trains between which passengers changed at the junction, was easier to work.

In 1883 the rails were finally lifted from the Llangurig branch of the Manchester & Milford; some agreement had been made earlier between the Receiver for the M&M and the Cambrian, who had of course inherited the

Penpontbren Junction area with the Llanidloes & Newtown area. Faint hopes were still alive that use could be made of the branch, although by this time nearly two miles of rail had already been stripped to replace worn rails on other parts of the M&M. It was in 1883 that this company decided, not before time, to use modern steel rails, cost what it might.

In Britain as a whole, disused railways were rare at this time, and branches which had never been used much rarer. Curiously enough, as late as 1896 the map in the ABC Railway Guide still showed the branch to Llangurig, without indicating that it had never opened. The fascination which the formation and bridges of this branch still exercise was felt by T.R. Perkins, the railway historian, and in 1904 he went over to the junction with his photographer friend Fox-Davies, both on bicycles. The photographs taken, published in the *Railway Magazine* in 1906, show the signal box shuttered, the signals standing but a bit groggy, and the siding on the down side still *in situ*. There were still a few old rails lying here and there. The northbound line to Llanidloes had gone; it seems fairly certain it was never used.

This was not Mr Perkins's first visit to the Mid-Wales line; it formed part of his itinerary on a holiday in July 1900, lovingly remembered in an article he wrote 51 years later for the magazine *Railways*. We can pick up his odyssey as he finds the Midland Railway train to Swansea in the north bay at Hereford; it comprises a Johnson 0–4–4T with several six-wheelers, and they set off, taking a sharp turn on to Midland metals. At Hay he records that the Golden Valley Railway was derelict (though it was open again later). At Three Cocks in true railway enthusiast style, he remains in the train although he should have got off, and continues to Talyllyn to see the little red 2–4–0T on the Brecon & Merthyr train. Now he joins the Cambrian train, hauled by 'a small-wheeled 4–4–0, black with orange lining-out, and carriages mixed four-wheel and six-wheel with white upper panels and green lower panels'. He retraces his ride to Three Cocks again, and goes on to Rhayader.

Next morning, he walks up the Elan Valley; the railway there is very busy as he plods up to Caban Coch. Still breathless from a smart trot back to Rhayader station, he climbs aboard the Moat Lane train (stock not noted), comments on the high moorland into which he enters after passing through the Marteg tunnel, and also on the 'several drunken-looking signals' at Penpontbren. At Moat Lane he joins a Welshpool train and is favourably impressed with Cambrian bogie stock — so the Mid-Wales train was non-bogie. After that he visits just about every railway in Mid-Wales; the last one is the Mawddwy, and he is unable to travel on that as his wife is coming on the next train to Cemmes Road Junction — a common experience for railway enthusiasts.

In the early 'eighties the Mid-Wales was a little stronger and felt able to put out feelers to the Cambrian regarding a possible take-over. Negotiations went slowly; the Cambrian was not itself in a very good state. When formed, the Board had been filled up with nominees of the various companies forming parts of it, and now there was continual bickering between the 'Coast Line' nominees and the rest. This led to poor management; David

Davies went so far as to say that 'the rails will shortly be sprinkled with human blood'. This angered the Chairman, the former Lord Vane, who was now Marquess of Londonderry; he was not able however to come up with a more original phrase than that it was 'a stab in the back'. It is perhaps ironical that when 43 years later much blood was spilt at Abermule, Lord Vane-Tempest, a kinsman and Director, was amongst the dead.

By 1884 the Cambrian was forced to have a Receiver appointed. The person chosen was John Conacher, the company's Secretary, and he turned out to be an ideal man for the job. He unscrambled the complex financial situation, converting a rag-bag of shares into one account, and disposed of some of the 'backwoodsmen' on the Board. Under his auspices, though no doubt with a strong shove from Benjamin Piercy, he agreed a formula whereby the Cambrian in 1888 took over the working of the Mid-Wales Railway; in effect it swallowed it though formal amalgamation did not take place until 1904.

It is not desirable to quote the Working Agreement text extensively, as most of it was of interest only to the lawyers of both sides; certain Articles can be picked out however:

> Article 4 — The Mid-Wales Company will not do anything that might disturb the exercise or quiet enjoyment by the Cambrian Company of any rights or powers secured to them in the Agreement.

> Article 11 — As from 1st January, 1888 the Cambrian shall manage the Mid-Wales Railway. (A later Article enjoins that the Mid-Wales will continue to run itself as agent for the Cambrian until 2nd April, 1888.)

> Article 15 — All receipts to be pooled except for income from Aberdovey Pier and the Llanidloes joint station and line, which will be retained by the Cambrian.

> Article 16 — From the residue and balance of gross receipts less payments, the Mid-Wales will receive 16 per cent up to a total of £92,000 per annum and 18 per cent of all sums beyond.

> Article 25 — The Mid-Wales Company shall on 2nd April, 1888 cause to be delivered to the Cambrian Company free of charge all their rolling stock and plant except three locomotive engines and some old rails and the furniture of the London office.

> Article 26 — Identifies the old rails as 'that portion of the Mid-Wales Railway which has not yet been relaid with steel rails . . . the length being about 1716 yards . . . which shall be sold or applied in any way so that no liability shall rest on the Cambrian Company'.

The identity of the three locomotives omitted from the take-over is discussed in the chapter on locomotives later in this book.

The Mid-Wales was to remain legally independent for another 16 years, but in effect it was now part of the Cambrian Railways and its chequered career as a railway in its own right was at an end. It had survived, but that is all; no branches had been opened, it had never owned either of its termini, it had generated no profits, it had not noticeably affected population growth in its towns. It is true that it had fulfilled its first task, to provide communi-

Mid Wales and Brecon and Merthyr Railways,
Worcester, Bristol, Bath, &c.
Via Llanidloes.

Left table (Down)

		a m	B	A	a m	a m	m	p m
Via Talyllyn	CARDIFF ....dep.	..	..	1030	1 25	..	..	..
	Newport (Mon.) ,,	..	8 25	11 5	1 20			
	Merthyr ,,	..	9 38	1210	2 37			
	Dowlais ,,	..	9 35	12 5	2 37			
	Swansea ,,	..	11 0					
	Neath ,,	..	8 0	1 20				
Via Three Cocks	BRISTOL ,,	..	9 10	1055				
	Clifton Down.. ,,	..	8 50	10 0				
	Montpellier ,,	..	8 53	10 3				
	BATH ,,	..	8 45	1040				
G.W.R. Midland via Gloucest'r	Birmingham(viaWorc'ter) ,,	..	8 45	1248				
	Worc'ter(Foregate-st.) ,,	..	1117	2 5				
	Malvern Wells ,,	..	1059					
	Great Malvern ,,	..	1137	2 32				
	Hereford ,,	..	1240	3 45				
	Hay ,,	..	1 27	4 32				
	Brecon ,,	7 15	1030	1 10	5 0			
	Talyllyn ,,	7 25	1045	1 25	5 10			
	Three Cocks Junction ,,	7 50	1115	1 53	5 38			
	Builth ,,	8 28	12 0	2 29	6 18			
	Llandrindod (Wells) ,,	5 24	1211	1211	3 57			
Via L.& N.W.& Builth	SWANSEA (Victoria) ,,	6 15	10 0	10 0	1230			
	Swansea Bay ,,	6 20	10 4	10 4	1234			
	Llandilo ,,	7 20	1113	1113	1 40			
	LLANDOVERY ,,	7 47	1136	1136	2 12			
	Cynghordy ,,	7 57	..	c				
	Llanwrt.d (Wells) ,,	8 14	1130	1130	2 39			
	Llangammarch Wells ,,	8 21	1130	1139	2 46			
	Garth ,,	8 25	1147	1147	2 51			
	CILMERY ,,	8 32	1154	1154	..			
	Llechryd Junction ,,	8 40	1228	2 45				
	Newbridge-on-Wye ,,	8 50	1240	2 47	6 37			
	Rhayader ,,	9 10	1 0	3 6	6 54			
	LLANIDLOES { Mid Wales.. arr.	9 45	1 45	3 45	7 30			
	LLANIDLOES { Cam. Rys..dep.	9 50	1 50	4 0	7 40			
CAMBRIAN RAILWAYS	NEWTOWN arr.	1025	2 29	4 50	8 12			
	Montgomery ,,	1048	2 46	5 30	8 33			
	WELSHPOOL ,,	11 5	2 58	6 19	8 50			
	Llanymynech ,,	12 5	4	4 7	25	9 16		
	Llanfyllin ,,	1245	4a50	9 55				
	OSWESTRY ,,	1147	3 30	8 0	9 29			
	Ellesmere ,,	12 3	3 48	9 51				
	WHITCHURCH ,,	1225	4 10	1015				
	Machynlleth ,,	1220	4 26	5 10	3 56			
	Borth ,,	2 0	4 55	5 10	9 25			
	ABERYSTWITH ,,	2 25	5 15	6 0	9 40			
	Aberdovey ,,	1 58	5	r				
	Towyn ,,	2 8	5 15	r				
	Dolgelley ,,	3 25	6 10	7 30				
	BARMOUTH ,,	2 45	5 50	6 30				
	Dyffryn ,,	3 3	6 36	6 58				
	Llanbedr and Pensarn ,,	3 13	6 53	6 53				
	Harlech ,,	3 21	7 0	7 0				
	Penrhyndeudraeth ,,	3 32	7 11	7 11				
	Minffordd ,,	3 36	7 17	7 17				
	PORTMADOC ,,	3 41	7 21	7 21				
	Criccieth ,,	3 52	7 30	7 30				
	PWLLHELI ,,	4 20	7 50	7 50				

Right table (Up)

		a m	a m	C	D	p m
CAMBRIAN RAILWAYS	PWLLHELI ....dep.	..	7 20	1020		
	Criccieth ,,	..	7 38	1040		
	PORTMADOC ,,	..	7 50	1054		
	Minffordd ,,	..	7 55	1059		
	Penrhyndeudraeth ,,	..	v	11 5		
	Harlech ,,	..	v	1120		
	Llanbedr and Pensarn ,,	..	v	1128		
	Dyffryn ,,	..	v	1137		
	BARMOUTH ,,	..	8 33	1158		
	Dolgelley ,,	..	8 10	1145		
	Towyn ,,	..	9 0	1233		
	Aberdovey ,,	..	9 8	1242		
	ABERYSTWITH ,,	..	9 0	1230		
	Borth ,,	..	9 18	1248		
	Machynlleth ,,	..	9 45	1 25		
	WHITCHURCH ,,	2a35	..	..	1 45	
	Ellesmere ,,	3a 5	..	..	2 5	
	OSWESTRY ,,	3 35	8 20	..	2 25	
	Llanfyllin ,,	..	7 50	..	1 30	
	Llanymynech ,,	3 55	8 36	..	2 37	
	WELSHPOOL ,,	4 40	9 10	..	3 0	
	Montgomery ,,	4 56	9 25	..	r	
	NEWTOWN ,,	5 17	9 50	..	3 26	
	LLANIDLOES { Cam. Rys. arr.	6 5	11 5	..	3 56	
	LLANIDLOES { Mid Wales. dep.	6 8	1110	3 0	4 25	
	Rhayader arr.	6 42	1145	3 40	5 3	
Via Builth L.&N.W.	Newbridge-on-Wyo ,,	7 0	12 5	..	5 23	
	Llechryd Junction ,,	7 9	1215	4	5 33	
	Llandrindod (Wells) ,,	8 58	1250	..	7 43	
	CILMERY ,,	9 45	1235	..	8 16	
	Garth ,,	9 54	1235	..	8 24	
	Llangammarch Wells ,,	10 0	1240	4 28	8 30	
	Llanwrtyd (Wells) ,,	1010	1248	4 35	8 38	
	Cynghordy ,,	1025	1 2	..	8 54	
	LLANDOVERY ,,	1035	1 12	5 0	9 5	
	Llandilo ,,	1112	1 34	5 22	9 28	
	Swansea Bay ,,	1216	2 41	6 20	1020	
	SWANSEA (Victoria) ,,	1255	2 45	6 25	1025	
	Builth ,,	7 18	1245	4 18	5 45	
	Three Cocks Junction ,,	7 48	1 30	4 48	6 20	
	Talyllyn ,,	8 20	2 10	5 18	6 45	
	Brecon ,,	8 33	2 25	5 25	6 55	
Via Three Cocks	Hay ,,	8 5	2 9	..	7 35	
	Hereford ,,	9 0	2 57	..	7 35	
Midland via Gloucest'r G.W.R.	Malvern Wells ,,	1057	6	..	8 47	
	Great Malvern ,,	1044	4 44	..	8 52	
	Worc'ter(Foregate-st) ,,	11 8	5 0	..	9 14	
	Birmingham(viaWorc'ter) ,,	1 10	6 15	..	1028	
	BATH ,,	2 20	8 20	..		
	Montpellier ,,	2 12	8 6	..		
	Clifton Down.. ,,	2 15	8 10	..		
	BRISTOL ,,	2 5	8 0	..	1130	
Via Talyllyn	Neath ,,	3 50	7 32	..		
	Swansea ,,	1 29	..			
	Dowlais ,,	9 20	3 20	6 20		
	Merthyr ,,	9 42	3 30	6 28		
	Newport (Mon.) ,,	1031	4 45	7 45		
	CARDIFF ,,	1149	5 4			

a—Except Mondays from Whitchurch and Ellesmere. c—Stops if required. r—Stops to set down on n tice being given by the passenger to the Guard at the preceding stopping station, or by signal for 1st and 2nd class passengers to or from local stations, and 1st, 2nd, and 3rd class to and from stations on other Companies' Lines. v—Stops by Signal to pick up Passengers for Llanidloes, Welshpoool, and Stations beyond.

Through carriages run as under:—

A—Newport and Hereford to Aberystwith.
B—Merthyr to Aberystwith.
C—Aberystwith to Hereford, and Newport.
D—Aberystwith to Merthyr.

Passenger timetable for September 1886 showing through services from the Brecon & Merthyr, Midland, Great Western and London & North Western Railways via the Mid-Wales Railway to Cambrian stations.

cation between South Wales and the north, though it now had no monopoly
of that. But in their own small way the trains running through the rock
gorges and over the spidery viaducts were a monument to man's
determination.

During its independent days the Mid-Wales did not alter its basic service
from three trains per day each way down the whole line. There were in
addition short workings from Builth Wells, and sometimes other stations
south, to Llechryd to make connection with the Central Wales line trains.
This station, or rather what was after 1950 'Low Level', was not renamed
Builth Road until after the Cambrian took over. The early timetables of the
Mid-Wales Railway showed Dowlais (and Merthyr when opened) as if they
were its own stations; in fact all stations from Talyllyn to Dowlais Top and
Merthyr were listed, though not Pontsticill Junction where the train must
have divided. A morning train extra to the three mentioned above starting
from Llechryd was given a five minute connection at Talyllyn to the B&M
southbound train. At Three Cocks it passed a similar train going the other
way.

Arrangements at the north end with the Cambrian Railway were not very
helpful for passengers, who had in any case to face changing trains at both
Moat Lane and Llanidloes. There was a fast train at 6.30 am from Moat Lane
connecting off the 4.40 fast from Welshpool to Aberystwyth, but a 45 minute
wait was required at Llanidloes. Through passengers to South Wales had to
wait for two hours either at Builth Wells or elsewhere to pick up the extra
train mentioned above. From 15th May, 1866 the Mid-Wales was appointed
to carry mails, and the evening 'Mail' from Brecon reached Llanidloes in 2
hours 10 minutes. This had an instant connection to Oswestry, but one
wonders whether the Cambrian held their train if the Mid-Wales one was
late. There was no other train over the Cambrian, so a late-running train from
Brecon probably meant business for Llanidloes hotel-keepers.

No trains were booked to stop at Aberedw or Tylwch, and one missed out
Erwood. All regular passenger train passings were at Builth Wells or Three
Cocks.

The company had never based its expectations solely on local traffic, and
in 1874, as stated above, a thrice-weekly service was begun from Llanidloes
to Neath; a Mid-Wales engine worked through to Neath. From 1880 in
summer time through carriages were run from Cardiff over the Rhymney
Railway via Bargoed and on over the B&M to Talyllyn Junction, then over
the Mid-Wales and Cambrian to Aberystwyth. Mid-Wales carriages were
also kept at Cardiff (Queen St) and Newport (High Street). Much of this
traffic went through to Cambrian Railway resorts, but some was for Llandrindod Wells, and this was handled by arranging connecting trains at
Llechryd, with the Central Wales (now LNWR).

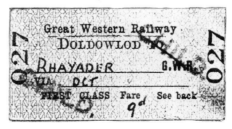

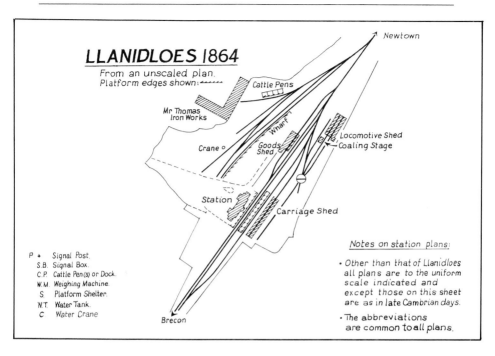

LLANIDLOES 1864

From an unscaled plan.
Platform edges shown:╍╍╍╍

Newtown

Cattle Pens

Mr Thomas
Iron Works

Wharf

Crane ○

Goods
Shed

Locomotive Shed
Coaling Stage

Station

Carriage Shed

P ✦   Signal Post.
S.B.   Signal Box.
C.P.   Cattle Pen(s) or Dock.
W.M.   Weighing Machine.
S   Platform Shelter.
W.T.   Water Tank.
C   Water Crane

Brecon

Notes on station plans:

• Other than that of Llanidloes
  all plans are to the uniform
  scale indicated and
  except those on this sheet
  are as in late Cambrian days.

• The abbreviations
  are common to all plans.

A 1904 view of the large elegant buildings at Llanidloes station.   *Lens of Sutton*

LLANIDLOES STATION

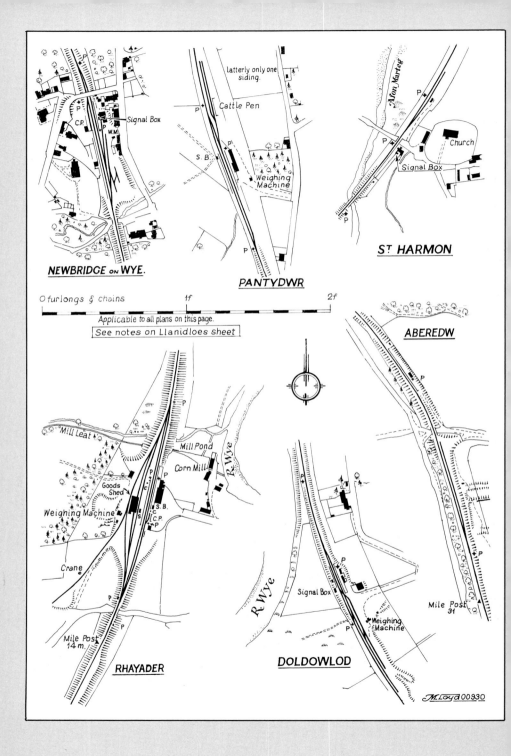

NEWBRIDGE on WYE.

Signal Box

C.P.

P

W.M.

PANTYDWR

latterly only one siding.

Cattle Pen

P

S.B.

Weighing Machine

P

P

St HARMON

Afon Marteg

P

P

Church

Signal Box

0 furlongs & chains   1f   2f

Applicable to all plans on this page.

See notes on Llanidloes sheet

ABEREDW

P

RHAYADER

Mill Leat

Mill Pond

Corn Mill

R. Wye

Goods Shed

P

Weighing Machine

S.B.

S

C.P.

P

Crane

P

P

Mile Post 14 m.

DOLDOWLOD

R. Wye

Signal Box

P

Weighing Machine

P

Mile Post 31

M. Lloyd 00930

The diminutive wooden station buildings of Doldowlod station as seen in 1904.
Oakwood Press

A view of Rhayader station in 1900, the nearest station to the construction site of the Elan Valley reservoirs. *Real Photographs, Courtesy Ian Allan Ltd*

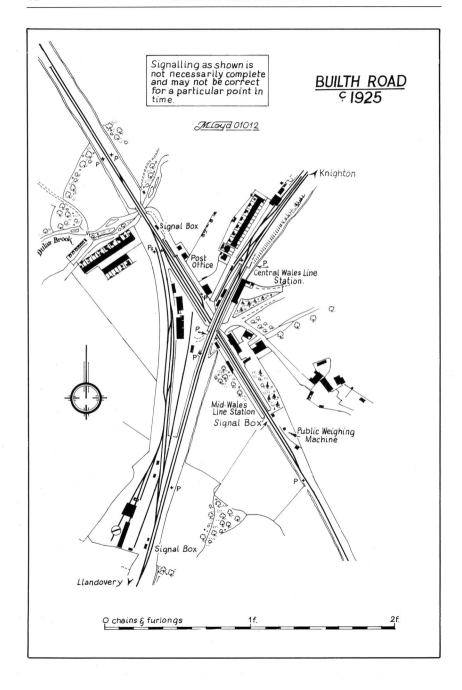

Signalling as shown is
not necessarily complete
and may not be correct
for a particular point in
time.

M.Loyd 01012

BUILTH ROAD
c 1925

Knighton

Signal Box

Dulas Brook

Post
Office

P

Central Wales Line
Station.

Mid-Wales
Line Station
Signal Box

Public Weighing
Machine

Signal Box

Llandovery

O chains & furlongs   1f.   2f.

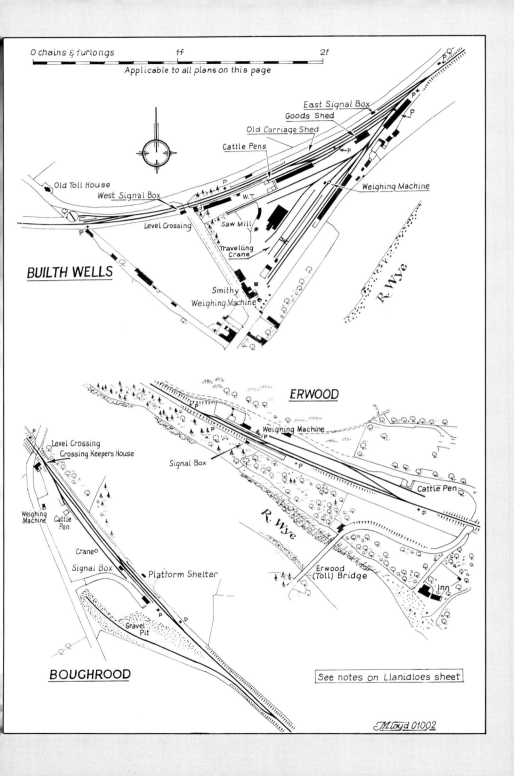

0 chains & furlongs 1f 2f

Applicable to all plans on this page

East Signal Box
Goods Shed
Old Carriage Shed
Cattle Pens
Weighing Machine

Old Toll House
West Signal Box
W.T.
P
Level Crossing
Saw Mill
Travelling Crane

BUILTH WELLS

Smithy
Weighing Machine

R. Wye

ERWOOD

Weighing Machine

Level Crossing
Crossing Keepers House

Signal Box

Cattle Pen

Weighing Machine
Cattle Pen

Crane
Signal Box
Platform Shelter

R. Wye

Erwood
(Toll) Bridge

Inn

Gravel Pit

BOUGHROOD

See notes on Llanidloes sheet

J.M.Lloyd 01002

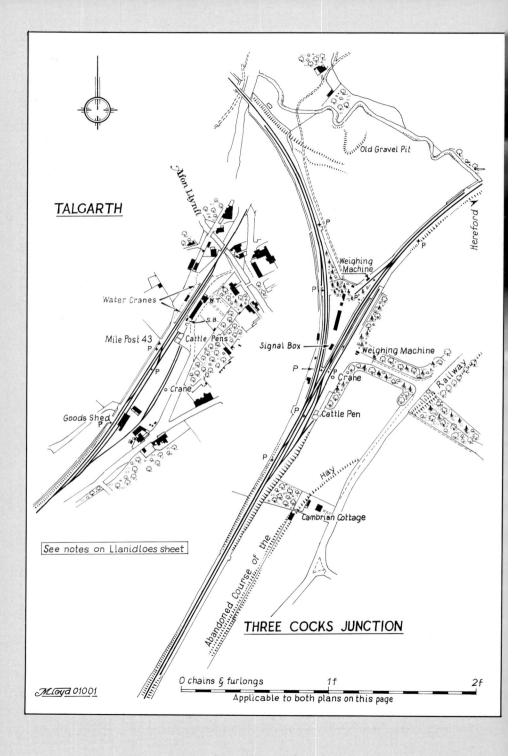

TALGARTH

Afon Llynfi

Old Gravel Pit

Hereford

Weighing
Machine

Water Cranes

W.T.

S.B.

Mile Post 43

Cattle Pens

Signal Box

Weighing Machine

Crane

Crane

Cattle Pen

Goods Shed

Railway

P

Hay

Cambrian Cottage

See notes on Llanidloes sheet

Abandoned Course of the

THREE COCKS JUNCTION

M.Loyd 01001

O chains & furlongs   1f   2f

Applicable to both plans on this page

A private owner wagon for the B.Q.C. quarry at Llanelwedd near Builth Wells, photographed in 1956.   *Courtesy I.L. Wright*

The '2301' class, Dean 0−6−0 was the mainstay of the Mid-Wales line for thirty years. Shown here is No. 2538, the last to work, with a Moat Lane train at Three Cocks on 13th September, 1956; a few months later she was sent to Swindon, withdrawn and broken-up.   *R.M. Casserley*

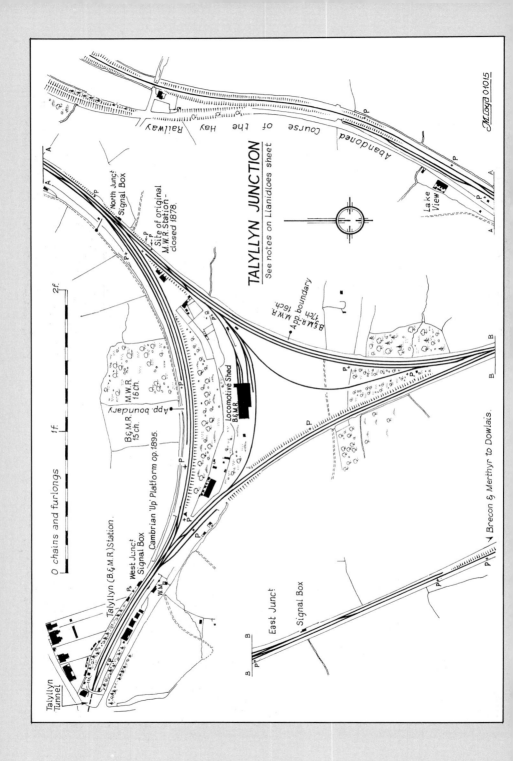

TALYLLYN JUNCTION

See notes on Llanidloes sheet

Abandoned course of the Hay Railway

North Junct
Signal Box

Site of original
M.W.R. Station –
closed 1878.

Lake
View

B&M.R.
17ch 16ch.

App. boundary

M.W.R.
16 ch.

B&M.R.
15 ch.

App. boundary

Locomotive Shed
B&M.R.

Cambrian 'Up' Platform op. 1895.

0 chains and furlongs

2f.

1f.

Talyllyn (B.&M.R.) Station.

West Junct
Signal Box

W.M.

Talyllyn
Tunnel

East Junct
Signal Box

Brecon & Merthyr to Dowlais.

B

B

JM Lloyd 0.10.15

This view taken on 14th June, 1962 shows No. 46511 crossing the River Wye near Boughrood station, with a northbound 2.15 pm service.   *Oakwood Press*

Erwood station looking towards Brecon. Note that the slip crossing allows up goods trains to set back to the goods shed at far left.   *Oakwood Press*

The station buildings of the early Mid-Wales Railway station at Talyllyn after conversion to a private dwelling.   *Courtesy Railway Magazine*

The station master's house at Doldowlod, now a private dwelling. Note the chimney brick-work and the platform edge of the loading dock in the foreground.

Oakwood Press

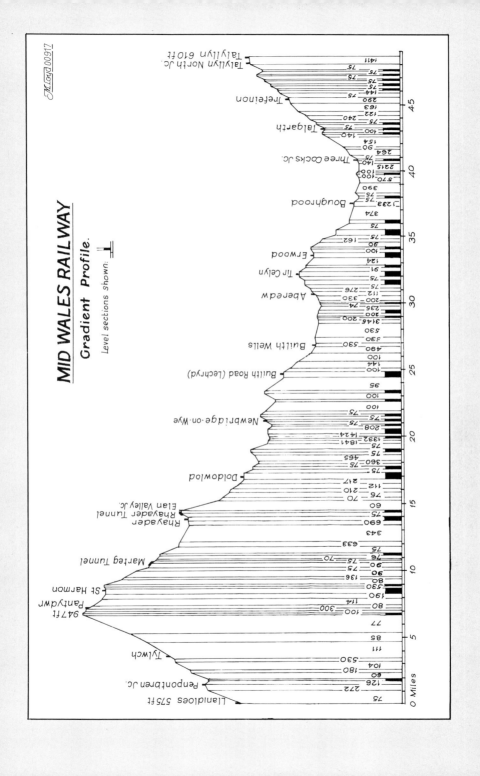

MID WALES RAILWAY

Gradient Profile.

Level sections shown:

The east end of Moat Lane Junction station, seen here on 26th September, 1962. No. 46503 is entering the station with the 2.35 pm from Newtown for Builth and Brecon. *Oakwood Press*

The Mid-Wales side of the triangular platform at Moat Lane seen in 1953; the Dean 0–6–0 has 'parked' the branch train and is seen running over the junction to go 'on shed'. *Oakwood Press*

Chapter Five
The Route Described

Before considering the history of the line after the Cambrian took over, the route itself and its stations will be described. For simplicity, any changes which took place later will be introduced here. There are three starting points; Moat Lane Junction, where the Mid-Wales Line later seemed to begin; Llanidloes station from which mileage is calculated; and Penpontbren Junction where the ownership of the line by the Mid-Wales Company began.

Moat Lane Junction, being less than a mile from Caersws station, served no purpose other than interchange. On the Machynlleth line the up platform was an island, and there was a bay at the down end of the down platform. The Mid-Wales side however had only one platform, with an engine release loop. In the 'V' formed by the two lines was a locomotive shed, entered from the down end of the Machynlleth line station, by the West signal box. The East signal box was at the up end by a crossover. The engine shed was rebuilt after the last War, and housed about six tender engines, and also the small tank engines used on the Van branch. This was a busy station in summer, with Refreshment Room in use, and its working could appear confused if there were banking engines to be attached or detached, and the Coast train was long enough to foul the Mid-Wales junction. The footpath to the station from Caersws village ran through the engine shed area, though there was a less direct way by a minor road. At the first level crossing on the Mid-Wales line there was the original Llanidloes & Newtown Railway Moat Lane station; this would probably not have been built if the present Caersws station had existed at the time.

There were two L&N stations on what later became the Mid-Wales Line, Llandinam and Dolwen; they were identical, with level-crossing and single platform, except that Llandinam had a goods yard, probably necessitated by the presence nearby of David Davies's mansion. Neither station was called at by all trains.

Llanidloes station was originally a few hundred yards up the line; this was later used only for goods after the large joint station for the L&N, Mid-Wales, and M&M was built in 1862–1864; this had a large brick station building with wings, a most impressive sight. The down platform was an island; at the up end there were two engine sheds, one for the L&N and one for the Mid-Wales. The latter was small, between the larger shed and the signal box; it was later taken down and the site used for a turntable; there had previously been a table south of the engine shed. A goods yard and cattle pens were at the north end, west side. In Cambrian days the station had a total staff of twenty-six.

The Brecon line left in cutting to reach open country on the slopes of the hills to the east of the Llangurig road and then ran into the valley of the Afon Dulas (sometimes also called the Tylwch). Here the road turned south, the railway stayed with the river and after just over 1½ miles was high above it at Penpontbren Junction, with the M&M branch to Llangurig running off to

Another view of Moat Lane Junction showing clearly the station buildings sitting on the triangular junction platform. Photographed looking towards Llanidloes in August 1948.   *H.C. Casserley*

The bay platform at Moat Lane Junction on 26th September, 1962 with three Engineers Dept Coaches. (*Right to left*) Nos. 14485, 14494 and W9951W.
                                                                                    Oakwood Press

A 1934 view of Moat Lane locomotive shed showing the two-bay hipped-roof shed and an ex-Midland coach standing behind in the Mid-Wales sidings.

Author's Collection

A 1960 view of the shed with the new building now in place. *C.L. Caddy*

An Engineer's trolley seen here passing the closed station at Llandinam on 22nd June, 1967. *C.L. Caddy*

Llandinam station, looking north to the level crossing; note the pipes on the right which were destined for the Clwedog dam project nearby. *C.L. Caddy*

A view of Dolwen station on 22nd June, 1967 with the nameboard missing and the platforms overgrown.   *C.L. Caddy*

A very early postcard view of Llanidloes from the south. The elegant station building, goods shed and locomotive shed etc. can be seen in the middle of the view.
                                                                                          Oakwood Press

Llanidloes from South

Viewed on 18th April, 1962, No. 46515 receives the right of way at Llanidloes station on the 1.20 pm to Brecon.   *H.B. Priestley*

Llanidloes station buildings and forecourt. This building was a beautiful designed construction and rather ample for the requirements of the railway. Photographed in June 1964.   *C.L. Caddy*

Llanidloes North signal box photographed in July 1965.

C.L. Caddy

A class '2', 2−6−0 on a Moat Lane local service seen here at Llanidloes. On this class of BR locomotive, the crew was well protected from the weather when runnng tender first. Note the bay window of the station building and the locomotive shed on the right.

Lens of Sutton

The far end of Llanidloes station looking 'down' in 1960. The double line under the bridge was originally laid to accommodate trains of the Mid-Wales (*left line*) and the Manchester and Milford (*right line*).　　　　　　　　　　　　　*Oakwood Press*

A GWR 20T brake-van used on the local goods service seen in British Railways days.
　　　　　　　　　　　　　　　　　　　　　　　　　　　Oakwood Press

Tylwch Halt showing the loop still in place on 9th September, 1949, photographed from the 1.30 pm Brecon to Moat Lane Junction service behind locomotive No. 855.
H.C. Casserley

Tylwch Halt after the passing loop was removed and signal box dismantled. The station building is now a house called 'Tylwch Halt'. *Oakwood Press*

Glan-yr-afon Halt as seen from the train in April 1962 with No. 46515 in charge of a local service.
H.B. Priestley

Services passing at Pantydwr on 18th April, 1962; No. 46524 approaching from Moat Lane whilst No. 46515 waits with the Brecon service for the single line token.
H.B. Priestley

Two 1950s views of the 'well cared for' station at Pantydwr, looking in the down direction (*top*) with a view below looking in the up direction. *Oakwood Press*

The level crossing and covered ground-frame at St Harmons on a dull day in April 1962.   *H.B. Priestley*

The small Marteg Halt was situated on the curve and was approached by steep wooden steps (*left*); seen here in 1934.   *Oakwood Press*

The down platform at Rhayader seen here in September 1949. The station building is now used as council offices. Note that the nameboard has added below 'For the Elan Valley Lakes'. The junction with the railway which was used in the construction of these reservoirs is half a mile further down the line beyond the tunnel. *H.C. Casserley*

There are no details to describe this charming photograph. Situated on the down platform at Rhayader, it looks like a group of local ladies setting out with collecting boxes for some flag-day in World War I. *Author's Collection*

A turn of the century view of Rhayader station looking towards Moat Lane. Note the water columns on both platforms. *Oakwood Press*

Rhayader looking again towards Moat Lane, photographed in the 1950s showing the large goods shed (*left*). The station master's house can be seen extreme right of the view. *Oakwood Press*

the west. The climbing had been at 1 in 75, but was almost level at the junction. There was now a nasty little dip and rise at 1 in 60, and then an easing as the line ran into a cutting after crossing the river; it crossed the river three times more before entering Tylwch station (3¼ m.). This was a very picturesque station, but did not rate any trains stopping regularly. It had a passing loop but no facilities for livestock, and the staff was only a station master and two signalmen. The small box was on the up end of the up platform, which also had the station building on it. The down loop was out of use latterly, it being an unstaffed halt from July 1939. The line passed under the road and through a vertical rock-cutting; two more crossings of the Dulas were needed as the line threaded the valley to Glan-yr-afon Halt (5 m) opened in 1928 near a former siding; here two more bridges over the river were close to each other, and the line was climbing at 1 in 77. The summit of 947 ft was reached near Pantydwr station (7¼ m); a summit not to be compared with the main line one at Talerddig. The station served a tiny village, and had a short siding with cattle dock at the up end of the down platform; the signal box was on the up platform. Here the railway passed under the Rhayader road twice.

The railway now left the Dulas valley and after cutting through some ground arrived in the valley of the Afon Marteg; there was a gentle fall down to St Harmon (8¾ m, sometimes spelt St Harmons), which had no loop, but had acquired soon after opening a single siding north of the road, which was crossed on the level, the station being south of the crossing, controlled by a covered-in ground-frame. This station was not opened until 1879 and became an unstaffed halt in 1936. The run down the valley became steeper, 1 in 90, and the Marteg was crossed twice in quick succession before running into the 372 yds-long Marteg or Gilfach tunnel. Half a mile beyond this the line ran under the main A479 road by a much-buttressed bridge, on the west side of which steps ran down to Marteg Halt after this was opened in 1931 (11½ m). Here was the broad Wye Valley which offered some easier grades. The upper part of the valley, north of Marteg Halt, would have been used by the second Aberystwyth branch if it had ever been built.

The line ran along the east side of the Wye until it crossed it by an impressive high viaduct at Cwm-coch, then stayed on the west side into Rhayader (14 m). It was necessary to pass the town on the west side, at a high level. The solid-looking station was up a hill from the main town and comprised two platforms, with the main building, water tank and signal box on the down side, and a large goods shed behind the up platform. A goods line running between the shed and the platform was joined at both ends of the station, forming an extra loop. The down platform, which was slightly further north than the other, ended in a cattle dock; in Cambrian days the station rated, in addition to the usual staff, senior and junior clerks and goods porter. The railway left the station on a high embankment, but soon plunged into cutting and a short 271 yds-long tunnel leading to the site of the Elan Junction established for the Birmingham Corporation Waterworks, which will be described later. Here there was a falling grade for down trains of 1 in 60; the branch signal box was on the right as one emerged from the tunnel, with the branch itself curving sharply right.

There was now a mile of 1 in 60/66 down to the Wye at the point where the Elan joined it. Just beyond at Cerrig-gwynnion is one of the quarries used in the waterworks operation; it lies on the far side of the road and the railway siding did not cross the road, the loading siding being west of it.

Doldowlod station (17¼ m) was in a curious situation, in that it was 2 miles from Doldowlod Hall and only a few hundred yards from the much larger village of Llanwrthwl. However, the latter was on the wrong side of the river, and the owner of the Hall was an influential figure. The station was on a level section of half a mile, and an engine was sometimes kept there to bank excursion trains and goods trains up to Rhayader. If such a train was going to fail, it would do so at Elan Junction; coming after some miles of easier gradients, the final 1 in 60 sometimes proved too much. There was a crossover and splitting signal at the down end. The station building on the down platform was wooden; the signal box was on the up platform. From January 1962 the goods siding and up platform were put out of use.

Nearly three miles south of Doldowlod came Watts Siding, on one of the few bits of level in an undulating stretch. At Newbridge-on-Wye (21¼ m) the platforms were staggered, the down one being north of the up, with the signal box in the middle of it and the goods shed behind. The brick station building was on the up platform. There were two main sidings, but coming off them were two short ones said to be too tight for engine working, and thus needing cables to be attached. Now a short rise at 1 in 75 was followed by a 1 in 100 drop down to the viaduct across the Ithon river at its junction with the Wye; this was the highest viaduct on the line and the longest, with five spans.

The railway now followed the curve of the river; at Dolagored was the Thomas Siding (23¼ m), and soon after came the spur line to the Central Wales line. The Mid-Wales line became double before the junction, and the spur became a loop. The Mid-Wales signal box was almost opposite the junction (called the North box later) and there were short set-back sidings on both lines before passing under the Central Wales station and into the Mid-Wales one (25¼ m). Although opened as 'Llechryd', from 1889 it was known as Builth Road, and Upper and Lower labels were attached by British Railways. The down platform had a luggage lift to the Central Wales platform at its up end; the ample station buildings were on the down side. Inside the triangle formed by the spur there were some Central Wales line sidings, the engine shed and turntable being at the south end of the spur, to the west of the main line. There was a second signal box at the south end of the Central Wales spur, which seems to have been called No. 2 box in GWR days.

There was now a short run down at 1 in 100 to Builth Wells station (26⅜ m), the centre of rolling stock management in MWR days, the engine shed and carriage repair shed being on the up side, down end; there was a water-tank on the up platform, beyond which were the station buildings. The North signal box was on the up side, north of the level crossing. The south end was equipped with a starting signal from the yard, as well as a splitting home near the box. In Cambrian times the staff here comprised a station master, four signalmen, two shunters, a guard, district inspector, two

A down goods train hauled by class '2', 2−6−0 No. 46571 seen entering Doldowlod station about 1960. Note the station lamps and concrete signal post.   *Oakwood Press*

A view of Doldowlod station towards Brecon, showing the signal box and the slip crossover which enabled engines waiting in the siding to join the rear of a train to bank it up to Rhayader.   *Oakwood Press*

NEWBRIDGE-ON-WYE. CAMR,

A 1920s view of Newbridge-on-Wye station, showing the dip in the down platform to allow passengers to cross to the up platform. In the 1960s view (*below*) we see a view of the up end of the station; note that passengers are now directed to cross by means of the road bridge. Engines were not allowed to enter the short sidings at the far left.

Oakwood Press

Builth Road (Low Level) station showing the substantial and solid construction of the station buildings on the east side platform in July 1959.   *H.C. Casserley*

A class '2', 2–6–0 No. 46520 passing through the down platform in July 1957 with a goods train. Note the nameboard; Mid-Wales passengers changed here for 'The Wells', Llandrindod, Llanwrtyd, and Llangammarch; the first was towards Craven Arms and the other two towards Carmarthen.   *T.J. Edgington*

At Builth Road on 16th July, 1959, showing the line passing under the Central Wales line platforms; note the luggage lift at the right to transfer luggage etc. to the High Level. *H.C. Casserley*

Builth Road Low Level Refreshment Room. Note the ramp to High Level and the lifthouse to High Level. Photographed in July 1956. *H.C. Casserley*

A view of Builth Wells showing (*left to right*) engine shed, goods shed, carriage repair shops and station viewed from the Llanelwedd Rocks in 1910, looking south.

Author's Collection

The up-end of Builth Wells station, showing the water tank at the left, and the north signal box beyond the level crossing; photographed on a rainy day in July 1959.

H.C. Casserley

booking office clerks and two goods clerks, three goods porters, a weigh-bridgeman and a dray driver. The station was at the north side of the town, now running west to east north of the river, really in Llanelwedd; there was a siding for Llanelwedd Quarries, latterly in the form of a loop; the line turned south again at Llanfaredd where a halt (28¾ m) was added in 1934.

Aberedw (30¾ m) was a single platform station with no loop and only a crossing keeper; a double siding south of the platform on the down side was closed before the station. It was on a rising gradient of 1 in 112 as the line climbed past Aberedw Rocks; the gradient stiffened to 1 in 75 to a summit at Tyr Celin, where there was a small private platform serving the house across the road from it. The period during which it was open is not certain; but there are reports of its use as early as 1872 and as late as 1950. The line now fell steeply to Erwood station. This was not happily situated as it required a walk of over a mile over the river along two by-roads and a bit of main road to reach the Erwood Inn; however it was necessary to site it there as the railway was still on the east side of the Wye and the only bridge was near the station. The platforms were staggered, the down one being to the north; the signal box was on the down platform and the building on the up.

The line was now falling again at 1 in 75; there was a short level piece where Llanstephan Halt (36 m) was placed, which opened on 6th March, 1933; this may also have been the site of Phillips Siding. Boughrood station (37¾ m) was renamed Boughrood & Llyswen in 1912; the latter is the larger village, but is across the river. The layout here was unusual; the waiting room and 'Gents' were at the down end of the up platform; the signal box was at the up end of the up platform, with the siding behind it, but some distance from the level crossing to the north, which had the station building proper beside it. The river now turned east and the railway crossed it on a lattice girder bridge of 150 ft span. Running now on the south bank, it turned south across the Afon Llynfi to enter Three Cocks Junction.

Three Cocks (40½ m) was a four-platform station in the form of a 'V'. It was named after a nearby inn, the village of Glasbury being about 2 miles away and on the wrong side of the Wye, as well as being already favoured with a station on the HH&B. The Mid-Wales Railway property extended for 29 chains towards Hereford on the eastern side of the 'V'. It was originally intended to complete the triangle here, and faint signs of a west-to-east curve can be seen near the bridge over the Afon Llyfni on the Mid-Wales approach. The station buildings lay in the point of the 'V', with the large signal box near the actual junction. Sidings on the east side of the station were reached by a crossover and slip crossing on the Midland-worked side of the station.

Three Cocks is one of a select few stations mentioned in literature, in this case the diaries of the Rev. F. Kilvert, a noted Victorian who lived locally and was constantly urging his pony and trap forward in case the train might be on time.

It is opportune here to detail the main deviations of the Mid-Wales from the trackbed of the Hay Railway. At the junction between the HH&B and Mid-Wales north of Three Cocks the tramroad was 15 ft above and to the east, rejoining at Pontithel. There was a small deviation at Porthamal, where the tramroad is said to have had a wharf, and a deviation of the tramroad north of Talgarth included a bridge over the Enig river; it passed through the town running NW–SE, whereas the Mid-Wales ran NE–SW, but the tramroad depot seems to have been in the same place as the MWR goods yard. A large deviation began 3 m south of Trefeinon, with a tramroad bridge over the Llynfi river. South of Langorse Lake Halt the tramroad route crossed the Mid-Wales one and passed north-west of the MWR Talyllyn station, ½ mile being used as an approach lane to it; at the tunnel mouth, of course, the tracks co-incided. There were many minor deviations, and only one-third of the Hay Railway trackbed was used as it lay.

Returning to the description of the line, after Pontithel siding (41 m), there was some climbing at 1 in 75 towards Talgarth (42¾ m), a more impressive station than most, with stone buildings on the down platform, the signal cabin and goods shed being on the same side. A large water tank was placed near the station building, and water points were in place on both platforms; the goods siding boasted a crane of six tons capacity. There were splitting signals at the up end, and starting signals on both platforms at the down end, where a slip crossing enabled goods trains to set back to, or run from, the sidings to either platform.

The railway was still climbing as it ran west of the main road, joining the Afon Llynfi a mile beyond Talgarth, following it past Trefeinon, a very remote station which as stated had a loop added after opening and also a second platform. It was not an original station; the only habitations were in a hamlet called Llandefaelog-Tre'r-graig, probably too much for the nameboard. The station was unstaffed from 1960 but did not become a halt. Just under a mile further on, the course of the Hay Tramroad diverged to the left, with a cutting and a bridge over the Afon Llynfi; beyond Llangorse Lake Halt (47¼ m, added in 1923) the tramroad crossed over the Mid-Wales to run on the west side. The halt was at the junction between the main road and the side-road to Llangorse village, and was more convenient for walkers aiming at the large lake; although Talyllyn station was slightly closer, there was only a poor track.

Climbing continued to Talyllyn North box. This was somewhat of a misnomer as it lay exactly east of the West box, while the actual 'East box' was south of both. Originally they were given numbers: No. 1 North, No. 2 West, No. 3 East. The line became double just before the junction, with a siding also on the west side; the double line used as such continued to the West box. To the south however (what was known as the east loop), the running line became single, with a Mid-Wales stabling siding on the east and a Midland Railway one on the west; from the Midland siding an extra loop ran past the Brecon & Merthyr locomotive shed (closed 1923) to join the west loop.

The original Mid-Wales Railway station lay in the angle between the east loop and the main line, with platforms on both, and the buildings here remained for a long time after the use of the station had been given up in favour of the joint one at the West junction. The west loop, that is the running line for Brecon & Merthyr trains, was also single after the West junction; although a second line was laid alongside it, it was only used for

A view of Aberedw station with No. 46519 on the 2.50 pm from Moat Lane waiting to depart on 16th April, 1962.   *H.B. Priestley*

Aberedw station looking towards Brecon, showing the single siding beyond. This was controlled by a ground frame, and was closed a year before the closure of the station.
                              Oakwood Press

A fine view of Erwood station looking to Builth in May 1959. Note the staggered platforms. *G.J. Biddle Collection*

Llanstephan Halt (the word Radnor was added by the GWR). This Halt appears to have been little used! *H.C. Casserley*

Two views of Boughrood station. In the upper view, (*looking south*) note the distant signal for the level crossing. The lower view shows how far the level crossing was sited from the signal box; the gates must have been manned from the nearby house.

Oakwood Press

Three Cocks Junction, showing the up Cambrian platform at far left, the island down Cambrian and Hereford platforms, centre, and the platform for the trains from Hereford to Brecon on the far right. *Below*, a closer look at the station buildings.

G.J. Biddle Collection

Three Cocks Junction, (Cambrian Railways).

A period postcard view of Three Cocks Junction, posted in 1908. The publisher of the card has written the supposed destinations on the trains (all lines in use). It is unlikely that the left hand train was going through to Aberystwyth or the up Midland train to Birmingham. The Cambrian engine is a 4–4–0 No. 68 and the Midland Railway engine, a Johnson 0–4–4T.

Author's Collection

Three Cocks Junction on the Midland side looking towards Talyllyn. Note the sidings on the left which were entered via a crossing from the up line.   *Oakwood Press*

Three Cocks Junction on the Cambrian side.   *Oakwood Press*

Talgarth station looking in the down direction. Note the large goods shed and extensive sidings, with a crossover for goods trains to run directly on to the up line.
Oakwood Press

Talgarth station looking towards Three Cocks; note the cast-iron water-column (there was also one for up trains), which were supplied from a large water tank situated at the far end of the buildings on the right.
Oakwood Press

The small station of Trefeinon, again constructed on the curve. Just two small wooden station buildings and a signal box controlling the level crossing.

G.J. Biddle Collection

Llangorse Lake Halt seen here looking in the up direction on 16th July, 1959.

H.C. Casserley

A view of Talyllyn station from the road (*top view*) above the tunnel, showing the Mid-Wales line turning to the left and the Merthyr line to the right. (*Below*) A 0−6−0PT No. 7736 on a train from South Wales to Brecon.   *G.J. Biddle Collection*

Talyllyn West Junction. The left-hand line was to Three Cocks Junction, note the extension platform beyond the signal box. The right hand lines led to the East Junction and Merthyr, but only the left line was the running line. Trains from Merthyr entered over the slip crossing (*centre*).   *Oakwood Press*

Talyllyn West Junction box on 11th September, 1959; the photographer is in a Mid-Wales train hauled by ex-Cambrian 0−6−0 No. 896, while 0−6−0 No. 2227 is waiting with the 12.10 pm ex-Brecon for Newport.   *H.C. Casserley*

The original Mid-Wales Railway terminus at Watton, looking east. It remained in use as a goods station till closure. This photograph was taken in 1958. *Mowatt Collection*

A view looking west showing the station buildings more clearly. Photographed in August 1955. *Oakwood Press*

Two views of Brecon Free Street station, showing the dominant station building on the north side. The spur line to Watton engine sheds ran off just beyond the signal box in the top view. The lower view shows on the right, the bay platform used by the Hereford trains.   *Oakwood Press*

shunting purposes. Entering the station jointly used by the Brecon & Merthyr, Mid-Wales and Midland Railways, on the right before passing the West box lay the 'extension platform', erected in 1895 to enable a Moat Lane or Hereford train to be in the station without preventing a B&M train from proceeding to the East junction. The three sides of the Talyllyn loops were in length, 31 chains (north), 33 chains (east), and 34 chains (west); 16 chains of the north and east were MWR property.

Leaving the station, and now on the former Brecon & Merthyr Railway, the train immediately entered the Talyllyn tunnel, a reconstruction of the 1816 tramroad tunnel; a plaque recording its re-opening on 1st May, 1863 was affixed as part of the 1951 Festival of Britain celebrations.

Although the Mid-Wales was only a user of the station at Brecon, the layout there should be mentioned. Approaching from Talyllyn, at Heol Lladron Junction the old line went off at the left to the sidings and sheds of Watton depot, the passenger terminus until 1871; one platform remained there until closing. The high level line had some carriage sidings on the south side. The Free Street station itself comprised a large brick building on the north side platform, having a short bay at the east end, and a spur to a turntable at the west end. The other platform was an island; the signal box stood half way down the outer line, and by the box what was called 'the straight siding' ran down a long sloping spur to the west end of Watton depot, forming in effect a loop at a lower level than the main line. There were no watering facilities at the station, and engines finishing a turn would have gone down to Watton for attention.

LETTER CODE FOR MID-WALES RAILWAY RIVER BRIDGES		
Letter	River	Location
A	Dulas	½ m south of Penpontbren
B	,,	north of Tylwch
C	,,	north of Tylwch
D	,,	north of Tylwch
E	,,	south of Tylwch
F	,,	north of Glan-yr-Afon
G	,,	south of Glan-yr-Afon
H	,,	south of Glan-yr-Afon
I	Marteg	Pantydwr
J	,,	St Harmons
K	,,	east of Marteg tunnel
L	,,	east of Marteg tunnel
M	Wye	at Aber Marteg
N	,,	south of Rhayader
O	,,	Doldowlod
P	,,	Newbridge
Q	Ithon	at confluence with Wye
R	Iboway	1 m north of Llanstephan
S	Wye	Boughrood
T	Llynfi	Trefeinon

The centre column of the 'A' bridge over the Dulas near Penpontbren Junction, (illustrating the way in which the high bridge supports were made up from standard pillars, stretchers and cross-bracing; 14th July, 1962.
C.C. Green

The viaduct over the Ithon River where it joins the River Wye, after the piers were cased in concrete, about 1920. The northbound train is headed by a 'Beaconsfield' class 4−4−0.
Author's Collection

MID WALES SECTION. — MOAT LANE, LLANIDLOES, RHAYADER, BUILTH WELLS, BRECON, &c.

DOWN.	WEEK DAYS. a.m. (Workmen's Train. Mondays only.)	H a.m.	a.m. (Fridays only.)	a.m.	a.m	noon (Runs during June only.)	p.m.	p.m.	p.m
Moat Lane Jun. dep		5 5			10 15			12 35	
Llandinam ... ,,		*			10 20			12 40	
Dolwen ... ... ,,		*			10 27			12 47	
Llanidloes arr		5 25			10 35			12 55	
Llanidloes dep	5 15	5 27			10 38				
Tylwch .. ... ,,		5 35			10 46				
Pantydwr ... ,,		5 45			10 56				
St. Harmons... ,,		*			11 1				
Rhayader ... ,,	5 45	6 2			11 15				
Doldowlod ... ,,		6 9			11 22				
Newbridge-on-Wye ,,		6 18			11 33				
Builth Road arr		6 27			11 42				
Builth Road dep		6 29		9 35	11 45		12 25		1 5
Builth Wells arr		6 33		9 39	11 50		12 30		1 10
Builth Wells dep		6 35		9 40		12 0			1 12
Aberedw ... ,,		*		*					1 21
Erwood ... ... ,,		6 50		9 55					1 27
Boughrood ... ,,		7 2		10 5					1 37
Three Cocks Jun. arr		7 7		10 12		12 30			1 43
Three Cocks Jun. dep		7 9	10 15	10 29		12 32			1 52
Talgarth ... ,,		7 14	10 20	10 35		12 37			1 58
Trefeinon ... ,,		*		Fri.					*
Talyllyn Junc. arr		7 27		10 46		12 50			2 10
Talyllyn Junc. dep		7 35		10 58		12 55			2 15
Brecon... ... arr		7 45		11 8		1 5			2 25

DOWN.	WEEK DAYS. p.m. (Mondays only.)	H p.m.	p.m.	p.m.	p.m.	SUNDAYS a.m.
Moat Lane Jun. dep		3 10	4 40	8 25	9 20	7 50
Llandinam ... ,,		*	4 47	8 30	*	7 55
Dolwen ... ... ,,		*	4 53	8 38	*	8 1
Llanidloes arr		3 30	5 0	8 45	9 40	8 7
Llanidloes dep		3 35	5 5			8 10
Tylwch ... ... ,,		3 41	5 15			8 18
Pantydwr ... ,,		3 49	5 25			8 27
St. Harmons ,,		*	*			*
Rhayader ... ,,		4 4	5 45			8 43
Doldowlod ... ,,		4 11	5 53			8 51
Newbridge-on-Wye ,,		4 19	6 3			9 0
Builth Road arr		4 26	6 13			9 7
Builth Road dep	4 15	4 30	6 15			9 8
Builth Wells arr	4 20	4 34	6 20			9 12
Builth Wells dep		4 38	6 30			9 16
Aberedw ... ,,		*	*			*
Erwood ... ... ,,		4 51	6 45			9 32
Boughrood ... ,,		4 59	6 57			9 43
Three Cocks Jun. arr		5 5	7 5			9 51
Three Cocks Jun. dep		5 7	7 7			9 53
Talgarth ... ,,		5 12	7 12			9 58
Trefeinon ... ,,			*			*
Talyllyn Junction arr		5 23	7 25			10 11
Talyllyn Junction dep		5 28	7 30			10 13
Brecon .. arr		5 38	7 40			10 23

MID WALES SECTION.— BRECON, BUILTH WELLS, RHAYADER, LLANIDLOES, &c.

UP.	WEEK DAYS. a.m.	a.m.	a.m.	a.m.	a.m.	a.m.	p.m. (Workmen's Train. Saturdays only.)
Brecon... ...dep		7 25			10 40		
Talyllyn Junction arr		7 35			10 50		
Talyllyn Junction dep		7 40			11 0		
Trefeinon ... ,,		*			*		
Talgarth ... ,,		7 54			11 13		
Three Cocks Jun. arr		7 59			11 18		
Three Cocks Jun. dep		8 0			11 20		
Boughrood ... ,,		8 8			11 28		
Erwood ... ... ,,		8 17			11 35		
Aberedw ... ,,		*			*		
Builth Wells arr		8 32			11 50		
Builth Wells dep		8 36	8 45		11 55	12 40	
Builth Road arr		8 40	8 50		12 0	12 45	
Builth Road dep		8 41				1 5	
Newbridge-on-Wye... ,,		8 49				1 13	
Doldowlod ... ,,		8 57				1 21	
Rhayader ... ,,		9 8				1 30	2 15
St. Harmons... ,,		*				*	
Pantydwr ... ,,		9 21				1 43	
Tylwch ... ... ,,		9 31				1 53	
Llanidloes arr		9 37				2 0	2 50
Llanidloes dep	6 35	9 42		11 50		2 5	
Dolwen ... ... ,,	6 40	9 48		11 55		2 11	
Llandinam ... ,,	6 47	9 55		12 4		2 18	
Moat Lane Jun. arr	6 53	10 0		12 10		2 25	

UP.	WEEK DAYS. p.m.	p.m. (Mondays only.)	p.m. (Runs during June only.)	H p.m.	SUNDAYS p.m.
Brecon... ...dep	1 20		4 15	5 35	5 30
Talyllyn Junction arr	1 30		4 25	5 45	5 40
Talyllyn Junction dep	1 33		4 35	5 46	5 41
Trefeinon ... ,,	*		*	*	*
Talgarth ... ,,	1 46		4 48	5 57	5 54
Three Cocks Jun. arr	1 51		4 53	6 2	5 59
Three Cocks Jun. dep	1 55		5 5	6 3	6 0
Boughrood ... ,,	2 1		5 12	6 9	6 6
Erwood ... ... ,,	2 9		5 22	6 17	6 15
Aberedw ... ,,	*		*	*	*
Builth Wells arr	2 22		5 35	6 30	6 30
Builth Wells dep	2 27	3 45		6 34	6 32
Builth Road arr	2 31	3 50		6 38	6 35
Builth Road dep	2 35			6 40	6 36
Newbridge-on-Wye... ,,	2 44			6 47	6 43
Doldowlod ... ,,	2 51			*	*
Rhayader ... ,,	3 5			7 6	7 2
St. Harmons... ,,	*			*	*
Pantydwr ... ,,	3 17			*	7 15
Tylwch ... ... ,,	3 28			7 29	7 25
Llanidloes arr	3 34			7 35	7 31
Llanidloes dep	3 37			7 40	7 35
Dolwen ... ... ,,	3 43			7 46	7 41
Llandinam ... ,,	3 50			7 55	7 50
Moat Lane Jun. arr	3 55			8 0	7 55

†—Thursdays only.

*—Stops to set down on informing the Guard at the preceding stopping Station, and to pick up Passengers when signalled to do so.

‡—Mondays only.

§—Takes up or sets down 1st and 2nd Class local Passengers, and 1st, 2nd, and 3rd Class for Stations on other Companies' Lines, *via* Welshpool, Oswestry, and Whitchurch. Also stops to set down 1st, 2nd, and 3rd Class Passengers booked from Aberdovey, Llandinam, and Stations beyond. Notice to be given to the Guard to set down.

A—Stops to set down from Aberdovey and Stations beyond. Notice to be given to the Guard at Dovey Junction.

B—Stops by signal to pick up or set down Passengers booked from or to Stations on other Companies' Lines. Notice to be given to the Guard to set down.

C—Stops by signal to pick up Passengers for Stations on other Companies Lines, *via* Moat Lane.

D—On Saturdays leaves Wrexham 9.15 p.m.

E- On Thursdays arrives Llanfyllin 4.15 p.m.

F—Stops at Borth to pick up or set down 1st Class Passengers.

H—Horse Boxes and Carriage Trucks are only conveyed by these trains between certain points; particulars of which can be ascertained from the Station Masters.

K—Stops to set down Passengers from Aberdovey, Llandinam, and Stations beyond on notice being given to the Guard.

S—Saturdays only.

Cambrian passenger timetable for October 1904.

Chapter Six

The Cambrian in Charge

The Working Agreement brought no dramatic changes; indeed there was no money on either side to make new capital investment. One little local difficulty at the southern end of the line had nothing to do with the Agreement. Sir Edward Watkin, Chairman of the South Eastern, Metropolitan, and Manchester Sheffield & Lincolnshire Railways (MS&LR), a man not much given to compromise, had joined the Board of the Neath & Brecon Railway. During his term of office the five-yearly renewal of the agreement whereby the Midland Railway worked the N&BR between Brecon and Ynys-y-Geinon Junction, as part of its Hereford to Swansea line, became due. Watkin, who was competing with the Midland in Manchester, objected and a notice was published to the effect that these trains would cease running after 30th June, 1889. He forced the Midland to remove vehicles and other items from Brecon; he may possibly have had the right to do so, for the MR had an agreement with the former Mid-Wales Railway, but Brecon was not a Mid-Wales station. Anyway, the result was chaos. The N&B had very few engines, and none to spare for working to Brecon. The MS&LR sent down some engines and carriages, but it was such a shambles that the Board persuaded Watkin to retreat, and on 22nd July the same year the Midland was back.

A minor accident occurred next year, on 26th September, 1890, when a goods train parted and the rear portion ran into the front portion, throwing some 20 wagons down an embankment into the Afon Dulas. This was reported as being 'near the 'A' bridge 1½ miles south of Llanidloes', so it would seem likely that a coupling broke somewhere near Tylwch and the rear part caught up the front part as it took the short rise leading to Penpontbren Junction. While on the subject, the more serious accident at Tylwch on 16th September, 1899 must be mentioned. The down 'mail' train from Llanidloes had arrived, and it seems the staff were aware that an excursion train from the south was to pass here. However, the points at the down end were not set for it, and the excursion passed the home signal (not very visible at this point) and crashed into the standing 'mail' train. One lady passenger was killed; this is remarkable as a van was pushed half-way through a bogie carriage. The train crew and the station staff were all censured; the Cambrian later released photographs to the railway press of a van and carriage 'built to replace those lost at Tylwch', but it is likely they were rebuilt.

By co-incidence or not, the year after the Working Agreement was signed a matter came to a head which affected both railways to some extent. For years there had been a standing committee of Welsh railways dedicated to the creation of a through route from South Wales to Merseyside independent of either the GWR or the LNWR. This of course had been one of the main ideas behind the creation of the Mid-Wales Railway and the several abortive schemes which preceded it; however, little progress had been made to overcome the fact that north of Oswestry and Whitchurch all traffic had to use the big companies' lines. Now in 1889 the 'Welsh Railways Through

Traffic Act' gave official backing to the rather nebulous committee, and action began. The fact that Mr J.W. Maclure was on the Boards of both the CR and MS&LR and was very close to the great Sir Edward Watkin, who had just pushed his railway to the border by becoming a joint owner of the Cheshire Lines Committee Railway was relevant; so was the fact that Benjamin Piercy died in 1888. Piercy had been trying to get a through route over the Wrexham Mold & Connah's Quay Railway to a junction with the LNWR at Hope; now there were other plans.

The whole story need not be told here, as the effect on the Mid-Wales was not great; however it had started in 1882 when Benjamin Piercy came back from overseas and re-joined the Wrexham Mold & Connah's Quay Railway (WM&CJR), one of the members of the north–south committee. It was planned to connect the Cambrian at Ellesmere with the WM&CQ at a new station at Wrexham, and to build a new main line of that railway from Buckley to Hope. Later the target was Shotton, where an expensive bridge across the Dee would give access to another new railway to be built across the Wirral to Bidston, which was on a line into Birkenhead owned by the Wirral Railway. Unfortunately none of the railways closely involved had any money, but the support of Sir Edward Watkin and his friend Mr Gladstone was secured; the former's Hawarden Bridge across the Dee, named after the latter's Parliamentary constituency, was opened on 5th December, 1889. The new joint station at Wrexham was ready by 1st November, 1887, but building of the new Cambrian Railways' branch was slow, and it did not open until 2nd November, 1895.

The new railway to Bidston (which was absorbed into the MS&L) opened on 18th May, 1896. So an independent route from South Wales to Birkenhead was now open. It was a victory Benjamin Piercy did not live to see. In any case, as stated, he had strongly advised making the connection to the LNWR at Hope, but was overborn by the Watkin faction. Watkin himself retired due to ill-health in 1894, though his fellow-Directors went ahead with the creation out of the MS&L of the Great Central Railway, which did run some summer trains by the new route to Aberystwyth, but none down the Mid-Wales line. Some goods traffic came this way, but the two big companies were easily able to undercut freight rates in spite of longer inland lines. It was a good route on paper, as straight as you could get from Cardiff to Birkenhead, but the WM&CQ as well as the companies down south had single lines and fierce gradients. If the Welsh railways had not been underfunded, would this have made a good trunk line, or was geography always against it? There is no clear answer.

It was only a few years after the Cambrian took over that a large boost in traffic was brought about by the decision of the Birmingham Corporation to build dams up the Elan valley to supply their rapidly expanding water needs. Thirty years earlier an engineer called James Mansergh had worked on the construction of the Mid-Wales line, and noted the Elan Valley as having all the features required for water-storage. The Water Committee of the Birmingham Corporation got to hear of this, but took no action at the time. Twenty years later, with the water supply situation becoming desperate, they brought out the papers and commissioned Mansergh to

Rebuilt ex-Cambrian Railway No. 896 entering Three Cocks Junction from Moat Lane
Junction on 11th September, 1951 with the 12.02 pm service.   *R.M. Casserley*

A Dean '2301' class 0−6−0 No. 2572 on a train to Moat Lane approaching Talyllyn
North Junction on the north loop, passing the original Mid-Wales Railway station,
now a private house.   *Oakwood Press*

prepare a detailed feasibility report. In 1892 he was authorised to plan a series of dams in the valley and its tributary valley the Claerwen and one of the greatest projects in a great era of municipal dam-building had begun. It was the good fortune of the Cambrian Railways that the nearest station was Rhayader; but the area itself was remote and would require a private railway to reach all the dam sites. The whole story of the Elan Valley Railway has been told in a book by Colin Judge* (*Oakwood Press, 1987*) but it is necessary here to repeat some of this story to show the effects on the Mid-Wales line, which were to continue for some 25 years.

During the negotiations with the Cambrian, the latter endeavoured to have written into the agreement a clause to the effect that traffic to the dam works would be sent by the route most favourable to itself, but the Birmingham side would not agree. This was an attempt to keep the traffic off the Central Wales; a letter from the Secretary of the Cambrian Railways to his own Board reminded them that the Mid-Wales line was outside any traffic-sharing agreement with the LNWR. He actually referred to 'the Mid-Wales section of your line', perhaps forgetting there was only a working agreement. Had the Mid-Wales Company seen the Elan project coming when it negotiated with the CR in 1888, it would have no doubt asked for the profit from this not to be put into the common pool, on the analogy that the CR was pocketing all the profit from its own development of the Aberdovey wharf.

By October 1893 a junction had been made just south of the tunnel near Rhayader; however, setting up facilities for the intensive traffic which would develop posed problems. The Board of Trade would not allow exchange sidings at the point of junction, as it was on a gradient of 1 in 60, and it insisted on a loop and also a trap siding. On behalf of the Waterworks Committee, the Cambrian erected a signal box by the loop; a very large one, with 40 levers. It seemed excessive for a simple junction, but when it was designed the railway may have expected to be working some sort of yard from it. Actually, its only connection with the exchange yard as finally laid was one locking lever. The Cambrian offered to work the branch for the BWWC, but the offer was not taken up, although a short-term agreement was made for the Cambrian to work goods trains through to the Caban Coch depot, two miles up the line. The Waterworks Committee were right to decide to run their own railway; the works were bound to penetrate to gulleys and inclines where 'main line' equipment would not be suitable. A proposal was made, once the Committee had its own engines in 1894, to hand over goods trains further down the valley, but the place chosen was on a 1 in 40 grade. A Cambrian engineer went over the ground and suggested a yard be built at a point later called Noyadd, which was on level ground only 600 yards from the junction. This yard comprised a shunting neck with two sidings for incoming loaded wagons facing up the valley and two for empty wagons facing towards the junction.

The signal box and junction loop were opened in June 1894; the exchange sidings were not completed until August 1895. However, a Press and VIP visit had been run on 10th July, 1894. The passengers were picked up at

* The Elan Valley Railway by C.W. Judge published by The OAKWOOD PRESS

Birmingham, Buttington and Rhayader, and Great Western third class saloons were used. At Rhayader a change was made to old Cambrian four-wheelers, which were taken up the line by a 'Seaham' class 2–4–0T. The Waterworks Engineer had intended using his own new engines, but somebody informed the Committee that these were not fitted for continuous brakes, and it applied to the Cambrian for help. This was given grudgingly; the letter of agreement emphasised that the CR would have no responsibility for anything that happened beyond the junction. However, the Waterworks Committee had erected a station at what later became Elan Village, and all went well.

The method of working building materials and equipment to the site appears to have been as follows: a train would arrive at Rhayader, possibly during the night, and would be broken into sections to form up to three runs in the early morning up to Noyadd, by the 'Seaham' tank. It was allowed 33 minutes to run to Noyadd, set the train back into the arrival siding, release, and return to Rhayader for another trip. Some trains arrived from the Brecon direction and propelled up the branch; this meant that on running forward into the arrival siding, the engine was trapped until a Corporation engine removed the wagons, so an extra point was put in at the bottom end to avoid this. The working instructions suggest that the Waterworks only made one morning trip from Caban Coch to Noyadd, as a note stated 'the Cambrian engine, after putting traffic off No. 5 working (the third train up the valley) will run back to Elan Junction and wait there until the Corporation engine has put off and picked up its traffic and left for Caban. The Cambrian engine will then return to Noyadd Siding to pick up the traffic put off by the Corporation engine'.

The implications of this are that a BWCC engine could handle all the loaded wagons provided by three trips from Rhayader, though the 'Seaham' could manage all the empties in one trip; this is not surprising as it was down grade apart from the tunnel section. The first Waterworks engines were powerful six-coupled saddle-tanks by Manning, Wardle and Hunslet, which with their small wheels would certainly handle more wagons than a 'Seaham'. The engineer in charge for the Cambrian seems to have realised that this class was underpowered, and applied to Oswestry for a 4–4–0T to be supplied. It was generally agreed that six-coupled tender engines could not work on the branch.

The Waterworks railway ended up with a total of eight engines. Workmen were first carried in open wagons, but after complaints the Committee bought six old four-wheelers from the GWR, five thirds and one first. Later six more were purchased, and at least five from the Cambrian Railways. The wagon stock comprised low-side open wagons, small closed gunpowder vans, a lot of inside-bearing tippers, and an ex-Mid-Wales Railway guard's van.

Most of the 500 workers at the dam sites lived all the time in Elan Village, but some had homes in Llanidloes, and for them a workmen's train was put on by the Cambrian early on Monday morning, running non-stop to Rhayader; also a similar return train ran on Saturday afternoons. It is believed to have comprised two four-wheeled carriages roughly painted up and reserved for this job, possibly third class carriages Nos. 26/28 of 1860. It was about three miles from Rhayader station to the point where internal workmen's trains left for the various dams, and it was suggested that the Cambrian train should work through to Noyadd and meet the Waterworks train there, but the Cambrian would not agree to this. However when the Elan Village school was established, and the 'paddy train' was no longer needed to take them to school down the valley, arrangements were made for this train to pick the Llanidloes workmen up at Noyadd; but they still had to walk there from Rhayader station.

The Cambrian had started cashing in on this great engineering wonder as early as 1893, running horse-buses from Rhayader to Nantgwllt; there were also many privately-arranged visits. The Institute of Journalists in Cardiff must have had some 'pull' with the railway fraternity, for when in September 1897 it wished to visit the dams, the Cambrian was persuaded to apply to the BWWC for permission to run their train straight through to Caban Coch, though it probably had to run past the junction into Rhayader to put the journalists into the obligatory four-wheeled carriages.

The greatest day of course was the visit of King Edward VII to open officially the dams on 21st July, 1904. The Birmingham 'big-wigs' arrived first at Rhayader in several trains of GWR and LNWR saloons; the historian T.R. Perkins described the scene belatedly but graphically in the 1907 *Railway Magazine*. 'As each special drew into the station, there emerged from the sidings such a train as few of those present can ever have seen — a sturdy saddle-tank drawing a long string of goods wagons, each of which had hard boards nailed across to serve as seats'. As they started their journey to the dams 'there was a jerk which dislodged hats and threw passengers into each others' arms as the couplings pulled together'. It would appear that when Royalty beckoned, nothing was impossible; here were engines not fitted for continuous brakes pulling long trains of loose-coupled 'carriages' down a 1 in 60 incline starting with a tunnel and ending with sharp facing points!

Incidentally, this was not the King's first trip on the Mid-Wales line; as Prince of Wales he had gone down from Moat Lane to Talgarth on 25th June, 1896 to open a sanatorium.

The Royal Train of July 1904 seen here near Noyadd Sidings on the Elan Valley line with *Calettwr* (with smoke arrester) at its head. The Shropshire Light Infantry can be seen lining the track side (supposedly every 15 ft) and 'presenting arms' as the King passed.   *LGRP, Courtesy David & Charles*

The Royal Train left Swansea picturesquely behind two spotless LNWR Webb 2−4−2T engines. After using the connection at Builth Road, the train pulled into Rhayader and the King swapped his 1901 LNWR Royal saloon for lesser luxury. The BWCC and the Cambrian had arranged a Royal Train comprising 1st/2nd Composite No. 34 of 1861, First Saloons Nos. 9 and 11 of 1889, and full Brake No. 31 of 1861; all were four-wheeled, and the King rode in No. 9, which curiously enough was also used ten years later by his eldest son when he opened the soapworks at Port Sunlight. The programme was running late, because the Cambrian 4−4−0 No. 83 which had taken over at Builth Road had been unable to get the train past Elan Junction without summoning assistance.

The accounts do not make it absolutely clear that a Waterworks engine took over the Royal Train in Rhayader station, but it seems likely, as His Majesty would not have wished to halt at Noyadd for an engine change. Anyway, the engine *Calettwr* took the train up to the Craig Goch Dam, after a luncheon pause in a marqueed field at Nant-madog, outside Elan Village. All the elaborate formalities ran their course, and the King arrived back at Rhayader for the comfort of his large saloon, which left for Welshpool at once, arriving there an hour late. Local legend has it that this hour was later made up by the LNWR on the run from Shrewsbury to Euston, but that seems rather unlikely.

When the Royal Train had drawn off towards Moat Lane, the job began of sorting out all the notables' trains, drawn by a wide selection of engines such as never was seen again on the branch. But the 'scribblers' had gone, leaving nobody to describe the ensuing scene, on that summer evening of the Mid-Wales's longest day.

By 1905 the BWWC was considering running down the railway, which by now comprised some 33 route miles of track. All the engines were sold in 1906, and such work as was done fell to 'Seaham' class engines again. The Cambrian put in fairly hefty bills for the work, and these were queried by the Birmingham Corporation. The answer was tortuous and probably more easily understood by a railway enthusiast than by a Councillor. The company admitted that the 'Seaham' class engine was being used at Builth Wells for shunting, and therefore was not brought to the line solely for the benefit of the BWCC. But if it were not for the waterworks trips, this engine could be replaced by another type, which could handle a wider variety of work. In other words, the Corporation was being charged for the inconvenience of not being able to use an 0−6−0 as station shunter at Builth if the company desired.

Traffic now being very light, the CR obtained permission to convert Elan Junction into a simple one-line affair, and this was done in 1908, the box being closed. The Committee did not look at the matter again (or so it appears) until 1916, when track repairs became urgent. They took advice, and were told that if they lifted the rails and took advantage of the present very high price of scrap, it would provide plenty of funds to relay it later if it was needed. So the rails went to make guns and tanks, and all that was left was the branch from the junction to Noyadd; this was probably lifted in 1917 though no record has been found.

When in 1906 the Great Western Railway opened its great new harbour at Fishguard, the question of extending westward from New Radnor arose again. The line would have run south of the Radnor Forest, across the Central Wales at Llandrindod Wells, over the Mid-Wales near Newbridge, joining the M&M between Tregaron and Lampeter, with a new line from Newcastle Emlyn to Goodwick. 'The great population of the Midlands could take advantage of the shorter sea route to Ireland'; for once, there was no mention of American tourists. It remained a rumour until 1914, but nothing was done.

Apart from the excitement in the Elan Valley, the Mid-Wales line was enjoying a pleasant stagnation. Things were happening elsewhere of course. The Cambrian had woken up very early to the arrival of the motor bus, and in fact included in the Bill it prepared in 1903 for the final absorption of the Mid-Wales Railway, an unrelated clause giving it powers to run motor buses. However, when the first buses appeared in 1906, they were as a substitute for a railway extension the Cambrian had always wanted, from Pwllheli to the tip of the Lleyn peninsula. It would be many years before bus competition affected the Mid-Wales, even though at places like Newbridge and Rhayader the horse-charabancs soon gave way to the motorised version.

In 1902 the Great Western arranged with the Manchester & Milford Railway to run trains from Newport and Cardiff to Aberystwyth without change, and with some stops omitted. This probably did not impinge very much on the Mid-Wales line excursions to Aberystwyth, as most of its traffic came from the Valleys. It was meant more to steal traffic from the London & North Western service from Carmarthen to Aberystwyth via the Central Wales and Shrewsbury, which attracted passengers in spite of a longer route, by offering more comfortable carriages than the M&M bone-shakers. However this was only the start of the GWR invasion of Aberystwyth. In 1905 the Cambrian Railways had worked out a precise agreement for them to take over the working of the M&M, but while it was under discussion the GWR jumped in with a counter-offer, which was accepted. It was for less money than the CR was offering, but the bankrupt M&M felt safer in the arms of the GWR than in those of the Cambrian, which like themselves knew what a Receiver looked like. Also the relationship had always been soured by the failure of the M&M to pay for the facilities at Llanidloes, which admittedly it had never used. This problem was faced when the Working Agreement with the GWR was drawn up, and it was directed that the Llangurig Branch should be handed over to the Mid-Wales without cost. It may be over-stepping the mark to describe as a branch line one from which the rails have been removed; in any case the Cambrian declined to accept the gift, and after the final amalgamation of the M&M into the GWR in 1911, the latter was left with the job of disposing of the land on which the branch had been built.

From 1908 the livery of the carriages changed to all green (formerly cream and green) but this would have taken some time to complete. In 1912 the Cambrian's main line was doubled from Newtown to Moat Lane Junction; a timely move to improve the time-keeping of connections. Also in 1912

After the withdrawal of the Johnson 0−4−4Ts from the Hereford line, ex-Lancashire & Yorkshire 0−6−0s were among the engines which took over the service. Here No. 52525 is seen entering Talgarth in September 1951. *H.C. Casserley*

A fine track view in September 1956 of Three Cocks Junction station looking from the south. The Cambrian (ex Mid-Wales Railway) is exiting on the left and the Midland Railway straight ahead. *R.M. Casserley*

second class was abolished. It had been done before in 1893, but was restored in 1898 for through trains.

In August 1909 there was an arbitration between the Midland and the Cambrian, before Sir Charles Owen, General Manager of the LSWR, at Waterloo station. This resulted from long-running bickering which started in 1904 with a suggestion that the line between Three Cocks and Talyllyn should be doubled. The Cambrian suggested that the cost be recouped by raising the tolls paid by the Midland for passing over this line. A little later the Midland declared they did not require a second line, and instead a passing loop was installed at Trefeinon. In 1908 the Midland gave notice to terminate the 1878 Agreement on tolls and proportions of revenue to be retained; the arbitration at Waterloo contained no surprises and left things very much as they were, except for some adjustments in payments to the Cambrian on long-distance freight. Nominally the agreement ran to 1915, but as neither party raised the matter, it stayed in force.

The Midland was still running two through coaches each on three trains per day between Birmingham and Swansea. The *Railway Magazine* in 1906 took the trouble to publish some timings between Birmingham and Brecon; west-going trains took between 4 hours 15 mins and 5 hours 50 mins, and east-going ones between 4 hours 37 mins and 6 hours 10 mins. Average speed worked out at 18 mph which was not felt to be good.

Although the basic service over the line was still only three passenger trains per day, in summer time there was a good deal more activity. There were two through trains per day from South Wales. One left Merthyr at 10.37 am and ran non-stop to Builth Wells, although most of the time the engines were changed in the Talyllyn east loop. A second one left Newport at 12.05 pm and stopped at Pontsticill Junction to pick up passengers from Merthyr and Dowlais; then it also ran non-stop to Builth Wells. Both trains were bound for Aberystwyth, which was the chief draw for workers from the mines and steelworks of the Valleys; it is a pity that no enthusiasts left an account of a trip on one of these trains, telling us how they fared on the haul up to the summits on all the three railways they traversed.

Another source of summer-time revenue came from a brochure put out by the LNWR entitled 'Four Welsh Spas', with Llandrindod, Builth, Llangamarch and Llanywrtyd Wells featured on the cover. Special shuttle trips were run between Builth Road and Builth Wells for this traffic. It does not seem that the connecting loop was used; the *Railway Magazine* stated in 1910 that no passenger train had yet used the loop apart from the Royal Opening of the Elan dams — however this might not necessarily be true. Mr C.R. Clinker writing in *Modern Transport* in 1950 stated that through trains from South Wales to Llandrindod Wells had operated from 1891 to 1939, reversing down the spur. They were certainly given in the B&M tables as 'through expresses to The Wells and Cambrian Line', but the main target was Aberystwyth, and 'The Wells' might still have required a change at Builth Road.

The through trains to Aberystwyth continued to work over the B&M until 1915, and called for locomotive assistance from the Cambrian in most years, with one or more 4−4−0 engines shedded at Merthyr. It seems that from

1902–8 all the through trains were worked from Merthyr by the CR; from 1908–10 Taff Vale Railway engines are recorded working through to Talyllyn, probably on the train from Newport.

The Cambrian never attempted to run through trains from London down the Mid-Wales line, probably because such a train would not have been able to compete against the LNWR through train down the Central Wales. This was a portion of an express detached at Shrewsbury; it left Euston at 10.25 am and reached Llandrindod Wells at 4 pm. This was obviously a favoured train, for *Bradshaw* had a note against Newbridge-on-Wye stating 'Newbridge-on-Wye station is 4½ miles from Llandrindod Wells station'; no doubt a ride on a horse-charabanc and later the motorised version was preferable to a change of train at Builth Road. A reverse note was given in the tables against Llandrindod Wells.

Both the GWR and LNWR ran their best trains from London for the Cardigan coast at around 9.30 am, with minor changes over the years, both ending up at Aberystwyth as the same train at around 4.20 pm. However this train had no connection at Moat Lane with the Mid-Wales line, this having left previously as a connection off the 'North Express' from Manchester.

In 1908 the Mid-Wales acquired some extra summer traffic from an unexpected source, when the Neath & Brecon Railway announced a programme of special excursions to faraway places. For example, a passenger booking an excursion ticket to Buxton, then another very popular spa town, was offered the choice of six routes. Two took him over the LNWR, but two went via Brecon, Llanidloes and Ellsemere, and two others took the Midland route, passing over the Mid-Wales between Brecon and Three Cocks.

Tourist tickets to South Wales from Cambrian stations were also available by a variety of routes, even via Aberystwyth and the Manchester & Milford. Other choices were via Llanidloes, Builth Road and Llandilo, or via Llanidloes and Neath; those using the Mid-Wales route could break their journey at Rhayader.

For several years around 1900 there was a through coach in summer from Hereford to Aberystwyth, attached at Three Cocks.

There had of course been some improvement since the early days; if one examines the 1904 timetable, the early morning train from Welshpool required only a quarter-of-an-hour wait at Moat Lane, giving a 3½-hour journey to Brecon. The opposite train leaving Brecon of 6.40 am got its passengers into Welshpool at 10 am. But the sparsity of the service which still obtained caused frustrations; a passenger taking the North Express at Aberystwyth with the intention of travelling to Builth Wells would wait only 25 minutes at Moat Lane, whereas anyone taking the later London Express would wait for three hours! On Sundays knowledge of the timetable was essential; there was only one train, leaving Moat Lane at 7.50 am, arriving at Brecon at 10.23, and returning at 5.30 pm from Brecon. This made a good connection for the North, but if anyone for points west was foolish enough to travel by it, it was rather like the plains of the American West: the last train from Moat Lane had left 12 hours ago and the next train was tomorrow.

As time went on the timetable began to look busier, but that was illusory, for many of the trains were conditional: from Cardiff to Talgarth on the second and fourth Tuesday; Three Cocks to Builth Road on Mondays only; Talgarth to Brecon on Wednesdays only; Builth Road to Brecon on Fridays only; Talgarth to Brecon in school term only, to name a few.

There were to be no important changes until the withdrawal of through trains during World War I, which were only just beginning again when the Great Western took over. Their wartime withdrawal seems not to have been due to lack of passengers; the Cambrian was busily promoting holidays on the Cardigan coast well into the War; it was more likely done so that all possible paths should be available for the 'Jellicoe' coal specials mentioned later. When through trains returned in 1920 the Brecon & Merthyr Railway was at first able to work them through to Talyllyn, but soon Cambrian class '61' 4–4–0s or class '73' 0–6–0s were bringing them all the way from Merthyr; the B&M however supplied the banker often needed to surmount the 1 in 40 gradient leading up to the junction when running northbound.

In some years the through trains from the Rhymney and Taff Vale stations at Cardiff, which were joined at Pontsticill Junction, had the same engine from Merthyr to Aberystwyth. This had to be turned at Moat Lane shed; a long trip tender-first with much tablet-exchanging was not acceptable.

When war broke out in 1914, there was some initial flurry at Rhayader, where there was a Territorial camp, but the main army camps on the Cambrian were elsewhere, and it was some time before the Mid-Wales line saw any 'action'. When it came, it was due to the insatiable appetite for Welsh coal of the Grand Fleet at Scapa Flow. As anyone who has seen a film of 'coaling ship' on a World War I battleship will be aware, the tonnages of the stuff that had to be put aboard before going to sea were prodigious; the task of bringing it to the far north was also a headache for the railways, now under Government control. On most of the lines coal trains had to compete for paths with troop trains and urgent munitions; the Mid-Wales line may not have been ideal for heavy coal trains, but it did have plenty of paths. So they began to run, by day and night, being dubbed 'Jellicoe Specials' after the Admiral of the Fleet. Signal boxes were manned for 24 hours a day, and the restriction on the use of the heavy class '89' 0–6–0s was lifted. Although the length of train that could be worked was also limited by the gradients on the Brecon & Merthyr, they almost certainly would have needed banking up to Rhayader and from Doldowlod to Pantydwr; double-heading was not allowed north of Three Cocks.

The widespread cuts in rail services in 1916 when Britain began to feel its back against the wall could hardly affect the Mid-Wales, with so little to cut; but the Midland did have its through coaches between Birmingham and Swansea via Three Cocks taken off. The local council at Llangurig chose this time to discuss restoring and extending the old Manchester & Milford line via Llangurig; had anyone applied to the Ministry at this time for rails for any other purpose than being sent to France they would have got short shrift.

After the war the exhausted railways took some time to recover; however there was a noteworthy train on the Mid-Wales in July 1920 when King George V came to Talgarth to open the National War Memorial. From August

1921 the Cambrian was released from Government control, and in view of the soaring cost of wages and materials it faced an uncertain future. There was speculation that it would have to merge with a larger company, and the LNWR seemed for a time to be the most likely; but in the end the decision was made to include the Cambrian in the Great Western group, provided for in the Railways Act of 1921. This took effect in March 1922, in advance of most other groupings.

It is interesting that only two years before, the Great Western had inaugurated a new summer service from South Wales to Aberystwyth to compete with the Cambrian services via the Mid-Wales. It ran only at weekends, and must have been one of the most tortuous competing services ever devised, making use of the Brecon & Merthyr, Rhymney, Alexandra Docks, Taff Vale, and Rhondda & Swansea Bay Railways. The route was via Bassaleg, Caerphilly, Penros, Pontypridd, Treherbert, Court Sart, Llanelly, Carmarthen and Pencader, thence into Aberystwyth over the former Manchester & Milford Railway. It was 60 years since the Mid-Wales and the M&M had fought their battles on paper to reach that resort; now both protagonists were under the same ownership.

A view towards Brecon in September 1949 of Doldowlod station. The station master's house is in the trees on the left (*see page 48*).   *H.C. Casserley*

Mid-Wales Railway passenger engine No. 2, photographed here about 1896 outside Builth Wells shed with Cambrian plates on the cab side.   *Locomotive Publishing Co.*

A drawing of a Mid-Wales Railway Kitson 0−6−0 in original condition.

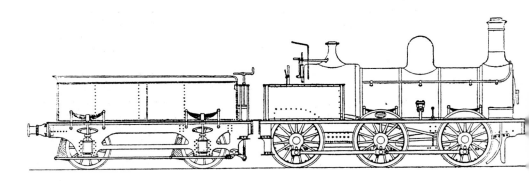

Chapter Seven

Locomotives and Carriages, 1864–1922

The locomotives ordered from Kitsons of Leeds, six 0–4–2 passenger engines and six 0–6–0 goods engines, did not arrive until a few weeks after the line opened, and it is probable that engines from Savin's stud were used, as they were on hand at Brecon. The passenger engines had 5 ft driving wheels and 16 × 22 in. cylinders, while the goods ones had 4 ft 6 in. driving wheels and 16 × 24 in. cylinders. Four-wheeled tenders were supplied. At the time of ordering, the company could reasonably have expected that one or more of the intended branch lines would come to pass, but in the event there was only one line to run, and on that three trains per day were deemed sufficient. It is not surprising that in 1866 the Board considered that it needed money more than engines, and hired out, and later sold, 0–4–2 engines Nos. 2 and 6, and 0–6–0 No. 10, to the Manchester Sheffield & Lincolnshire Railway. Similarly 0–6–0 No. 11 went to the Denbigh Ruthin & Corwen Railway, shortly afterwards becoming LNWR property.

The stud was renumbered in 1872, the four remaining passenger engines becoming Nos. 1–4 and the goods engines 5–8, not all in correct order. As related earlier, the company claimed at this time that eight engines were not sufficient to handle the traffic, and ordered two standard Sharp, Stewart 0–6–0 engines, which arrived in 1873, being numbered 9 and 10. These were the same as the Cambrian 'Queen' class, which Savin had favoured for the lines he was running; although their dimensions were similar to the Kitson 0–6–0s, (4 ft 6½ in. wheels, 16 × 24 in. cylinders), they were considered to perform better. However, this might not be the real reason they were purchased. For some reason the Furness Railway, which regarded these engines as their 'D1' class, between 1873 and 1875, failed to take delivery of ten of the class when they were built. The Mid-Wales could therefore have obtained them at a very keen price. Oddly enough, five of the ten ended up on the Cambrian: the two mentioned here, two bought direct but some time after building, and one which was purchased second-hand from the Denbigh Ruthin & Corwen Railway (DR&CR).

It was related earlier that three locomotives were omitted from the stock to be handed over to the Cambrian in 1888. In 1914 the *Locomotive Magazine* published a lengthy survey of Cambrian engines, in which it was stated that Mid-Wales passenger engines Nos. 1, 3 and 4 were scrapped in 1888. If one could believe that, the clause in the Agreement would have a simple answer. But it is generally agreed that all the 10 engines had Cambrian numbers allocated; also the above-mentioned article says that nine engines were handed over (it believed No. 1 to be already scrapped), and if three passenger engines had been omitted, there would have been only seven to pass over. The only possible explanation is that the three engines sold to the MS&LR (but not that sold to the Denbigh Railway) were either still on the Mid-Wales' books, or that the lawyer drafting the agreement misunderstood some rambling verbal explanation of why the company did not have all the engines it started out with. There is one other slight possibility; it is known that goods engines Nos. 5, 6 and 8 were cannibalised at some stage to keep No. 7 in action until 1904, and it is conceivable that the Cambrian regarded these as scrap in 1888, though their normally accepted scrapping dates were several years later.

The passenger engines were probably withdrawn between 1894 and 1905. The Sharp, Stewart 0–6–0s naturally had longer lives; No. 10 went in 1922, but No. 9 had a much more interesting history. It had been supplied with a new boiler and a six-wheeled tender in 1889; but in 1927 it was overhauled again and given a Belpaire boiler instead of the normal one with round-topped firebox, although it lost its six-wheeled tender. Five years later, it was decided to send it to the lightly-laid Lambourn Valley branch in Berkshire, and it got its 2000-gallon six-wheeled tender (or one like it) back again; it was not withdrawn until 1938.

When running in the Oswestry area after 1927, as Cambrian No. 908, old No. 9, attracted attention as almost the last engine in Britain to have a four-wheeled tender. This ran on a 9 ft 6 in. wheelbase, and carried 1200 gallons of water and 3 tons of coal. Mid-Wales engines were seldom worked hard, and there was a water-point at Builth Wells and at Talgarth, so heavy provision was only needed on the types of engine which might be sent down to Merthyr to come panting up to Talybont with a long excursion train.

After the take-over, the Cambrian put some 'Volunteer' class 0–4–2 engines and 'Albion' class 2–4–0s on the line, but in the 'nineties the 'Beaconsfield' class of small-wheeled 4–4–0 began to be used, and this type was closely associated with the line for nearly 30 years. These were designed by Alexander Walker, who had been Savin's assistant, and were a notable advance at a time when bogie passenger engines were rare. The first two came out in 1878, the first being No. 16 *Beaconsfield*. Improvements included boiler pressure raised from 120 to 140 lb., and cylinders 17 × 24 in. The coupled wheels were 5 ft 6½ in., very small for a main-line railway but suited to the Cambrian circumstances. With a weight of 33 tons they also suited the slender Mid-Wales viaducts. When William Aston took over the locomotive department in 1879 he continued the class, though only a total of six were built in all (Nos. 16, 17, 20, 21, 50, 60) before Aston turned to a heavier passenger engine (the '61' class) with larger driving wheels.

In 1899 Herbert Jones became locomotive superintendent, and in 1903 he introduced new types both of 4–4–0 and 0–6–0, both fitted with Belpaire fireboxes, and over the axle-weight allowed on the Mid-Wales lines. These were the '94' class 4–4–0 and '89' class 0–6–0; there is no doubt that at times of stress the latter must have worked on the Mid-Wales, but its axle weight of over 14 tons must have made such trips uncommon; the 4–4–0 engines were even more unsuited, with a weight on the driving axles of 15½ tons. The old 'Queens' were hardly up to modern loads, and therefore the ten class '73' 0–6–0s designed by Aston in 1894, and welcome on the Mid-Wales, regularly worked the goods trains and often the passenger trains also, especially after 1904 when some of the 'Beaconsfields' were transferred to the main line.

Before leaving the tender engines, mention must be made of two oddities which briefly worked on the Mid-Wales. In 1905 the Metropolitan Railway in London was electrifying its lines, and had a large number of Beyer Peacock 4–4–0T engines to spare. The Cambrian bought six of them;

however, though looking somewhat ancient (which most were) they had a rather high weight on the driving axles, and were restricted to the main lines. In 1914 two of them were rebuilt as tender engines in order to reduce this weight; they did not, however, become regular users of the Mid-Wales line. The various 2–4–0 and 4–4–0 engines bought from the GWR at the end of the Cambrian's independent days do not seem to have worked on the line either.

The Cambrian had very few tank engines; there were three 'Seaham' class 2–4–0Ts bought in 1866 from Sharp, Stewart; they were very light with 4½ ft coupled wheels and 14 × 20 in. cylinders, and instead of a proper cab they had a weatherboard bent over the top to join the rear of the bunker. They were later rebuilt and worked on the Elan Valley branch and at Builth Wells. The Aston 0–4–4T engines did not appear on the Mid-Wales apart from one visit at the Elan Valley opening. There were also a number of small shunting tanks obtained from various sources; a Manning, Wardle 0–4–0ST purchased in 1901, CR No. 22, was on the Elan Valley line in 1903, and No. 25, a 0–6–0ST from the same maker, was also used.

As rebuilt by Aston the 'Seaham' class had a larger boiler, higher pressure, and a proper cab. Unusually, the class was named after the last engine, No. 59, and not the first, No. 57 *Maglona* which worked on the Elan Valley. No. 59 *Seaham* was named after Earl Vane's son Lord Seaham and No. 58 *Gladys* after his daughter, examples of what some Directors called 'toadyism' which led to names being discontinued.

World War I put great strain on the Cambrian Railways' locomotive resources; there were big Army camps at Oswestry, Marchwiel, Lovesgrove

The 'Albion' class, 2–4–0 locomotives, built by Sharp, Stewart for the Oswestry & Newtown Railway in 1863/64, were later modernised and used on the Mid-Wales Line. This example No. 42, was formerly *Glandovey*.   *Locomotive Publishing Co.*

The '73' class 0−6−0 was used on the Mid-Wales Railway and this example No. 78, was built in a batch by Vulcan Foundry in 1895. This differed from the other goods engines in having large sand-boxes in front above the frame.

Locomotive Publishing Co.

Mid-Wales Railway locomotive No. 9 after its 1927 (*second*) rebuild seen here running as GWR No. 908. Here it has a four-wheeled tender but both before and later it ran with a six-wheeled tender. *I. Higgon*

(Aberystwyth) and other places; also munition workers with more money than they had previously were looking for holidays on the Cardigan coast. When the period of Government control ended, and the management had to face re-equipment for peace, they knew they could not do it. The favourite for amalgamation in the past had been the LNWR, but the Government made it clear that they wanted all the south and mid-Wales railways in the GWR camp. In 1921 the CR bought four old 2−4−0 and 4−4−0 engines off the Great Western, and the last two never carried the Cambrian livery; some Dean '2301' class 0−6−0s came to help out in 1920, and some 'Aberdare' 2−6−0s in 1922; it was a smooth transition, and it was the '2301' which would be the mainstay of Mid-Wales locomotive working for more than 30 years.

Great Western lines were classified for permitted axle-weight by colours, red being the heaviest and 'uncoloured' the lowest. The '2301' class was one of the few allowed on 'uncoloured' lines. There were 280 of them, built between 1883 and 1899; 50 went overseas in World War I (and a few did not get back); some of the class on the Cambrian lines had been to Salonika and back. The Army also made use of them in World War II, some being given side-tanks as well as tenders.

MID-WALES RAILWAY LOCOMOTIVES

1864/5 No.	1872 No.	Type	Built	CR No.	GWR No.	Withdrawn
1	1	0−4−2 Kitson	1864	22	−	1894
2	−	0−4−2 Kitson	1864	−	−	−
3	2	0−4−2 Kitson	1864	2	−	1905
4	4	0−4−2 Kitson	1864	24	−	1898
5	3	0−4−2 Kitson	1864	23	−	1896
6	−	0−4−2 Kitson	1865	−	−	−
7	7	0−6−0 Kitson	1865	33	−	1904
8	8	0−6−0 Kitson	1865	47?	−	c.1890
9	5	0−6−0 Kitson	1865	25	−	c.1890
10	−	0−6−0 Kitson	1865	−	−	−
11	−	0−6−0 Kitson	1865	−	−	−
12	6	0−6−0 Kitson	1865	32	−	c.1890
	9	0−6−0 Sharp Stewart	1873	48	908	1938
	10	0−6−0 Sharp Stewart	1873	49	909	1922

Nos. 2, 6, 10 (1864 numbering) became MS&LR Nos. 269, 268, 270. No. 11 became LNWR 2348 after the DR&CR was absorbed.

CARRIAGES

The Mid-Wales provided itself amply with carriages, perhaps hoping to use the many running powers it had collected. This stock comprised 24 third class, 14 second class, 8 first class, 8 composites and 4 passenger brakes. Almost at once, 17 were sold off, mostly to the Manchester, Sheffield & Lincolnshire Railway, and a few more later. Unfortunately there is no photograph known to the author showing what are undeniably Mid-Wales Railway carriages; however most builders at the time were supplying similar vehicles: four-compartment firsts, seconds and compos, and five-

A Kitson built 0−4−2, with the cab added and renumbered by the Cambrian to No. 24. It ran as No. 4 in the Mid-Wales Railway days being built in 1864 and withdrawn 1898.   *Locomotive Publishing Co.*

The Cambrian Railway 'Beaconsfield' class which worked on the Mid-Wales line for 30 years on and off. This was the first locomotive in the class, named *Beaconsfield*, built in 1878 with only six in all being completed.   *Locomotive Publishing Co.*

compartment thirds. The last were of square section and had outside body framing, with half-height partitions, and the whole vehicle was lit by two or sometimes three oil lamps in the roof. There were passenger full brakes (and a few brake thirds) of a similar design working on the Mid-Wales line before 1900; there was a door for the guard at one end, with a ducket adjacent, and double doors in the centre of the body (if full brakes). The Cambrian had brakes also of this type, and therefore this is no proof that the four full brakes of Mid-Wales origin were like this.

About 400 wagons were purchased: open wagons, lime wagons with covers, cattle vans, bolster wagons for timber, and brake vans. The brake van sold to the Birmingham Waterworks Committee had dumb buffers, and it seems likely that the other wagons may also have been similar; it is also probable that not all were braked, as sprags were widely in use for braking in yards.

The Mid-Wales carriages would have become mixed in with Cambrian stock soon after 1888; the three-compartment 3rd brakes noted in photographs at the end of the century were almost certainly the latter's. The Cambrian purchased most of its stock from Metropolitan or Ashbury, but some building was done in the Oswestry works. Six-wheelers were adopted from 1891 and bogie carriages from 1895; a few 6-wheel 2nd bogies had lavatories and might be seen on through trains from South Wales. Gas replaced oil lighting from about 1890 and vacuum brakes were fitted from 1886. Passengers did complain of the absence of steam heating, which was not fitted until 1912, and then only to main line stock.

An earlier view of locomotive No. 9 (Cambrian No. 48) taken about 1896 after an 1889 rebuild which included a new pattern chimney and Ramsbottom valves. This class had no engine brakes; those shown here were fitted after the 1889 rebuild.

Locomotive Publishing Co.

There were only three 'Seaham' class 2−4−0Ts built by Sharp, Stewart for the Cambrian Railway in 1866. They were completely rebuilt and in this form worked the Elan Valley Branch occasionally, when required. No. 58 (*above*) was formerly named *Gladys*. *Locomotive Publishing Co.*

The '89' class 0−6−0s were seldom used on the Mid-Wales on account of their weight. Former No. 102, seen here in September 1949 as GWR No. 896 on a down train at Newbridge, showing the new boiler and higher coal-rails which were fitted at Swindon in 1932. *J. Edgington*

Chapter Eight
The Great Western Days

The Great Western's first task was to breathe fresh life into the Cambrian's locomotive stud. Various ancient but reliable 2–4–0s and 4–4–0s were sent, but principally the '2301' class 0–6–0, which was soon strongly in evidence from Brecon up to Pwllheli. The Cambrian 4–4–0s went quickly; the class '61s' by 1930 and the 'Belpaire' class by 1933. Four of the 'Queen' 0–6–0 class lasted remarkably well, as light engines were required on some branch lines; No. 900 was noted on Machynlleth engineers' trains and may have been seen on the Mid-Wales. However, the Dean 0–6–0 was king from Moat Lane southwards, and would remain so for over 30 years. Nevertheless former Cambrian 0–6–0s were also often seen, up to the mid-'forties. The '89' class 0–6–0s lasted well into British Railways days, but were too heavy for the Mid-Wales line.

The Great Western also cut huge swathes through the Cambrian carriage stock, sending much of it to Foss Cross and other storage sidings awaiting disposal; the old Royal Saloon of Elan Valley days amongst them, now in drab brown livery. Many six-wheelers were withdrawn, though the replacements in some cases were Great Western four-wheelers. This was no doubt done because some branch lines found four-wheelers more suitable; there is no record of any on the Mid-Wales, which received a number of short clerestory-roofed bogie carriages for the local service, though modern corridor stock was supplied for the through trains, often mixed in with former Cambrian bogie stock, steel-panelled to preserve its life for a bit longer; in photographs their low arc roofs contrast with the larger Great Western outline. The Cambrian never built or acquired any high-roofed stock, apart from two observation cars rebuilt from six-wheelers at Oswestry in 1915, but only used between Machynlleth and Pwllheli.

By the early 'thirties, there were still only three trains per day down the line, but the timetables were perhaps more interesting. For instance, there was one train from Builth Wells to Builth Road which ran only when schools were *not* open; and there was the odd behaviour of the 9.15 am from Builth Road to Three Cocks, which ran through to Brecon on Fridays, but on other days paused for half an hour at Builth Wells before continuing to Three Cocks to hand its passengers to a Brecon-bound LMS train.

In 1931, *Bradshaw* indicated one shuttle from Llanidloes to Moat Lane and back, and the afternoon train to Brecon, as 'Rail-motor, one class only'. However no return train from Brecon was so marked. If this did indeed run, it would have been a motor-fitted trailer with 0–4–2T; although steamcars were working between Dolgelley and Barmouth they would not have been happy with Mid-Wales gradients.

A shuttle train from Builth Wells ran to Builth Road to catch the fast LMS train to Euston, a generous gesture, and no doubt a nice little run for some driver who spent all day shunting the yard. At Trefeinon, which handled both GWR and LMS trains, study of the calendar must have been essential for the staff. Taking Brecon trains only, the first stopped each day, the second ran only in school term, the third was Fridays only, the fourth ran

Great Western Railway

RHAYADER SPORTS AND CARNIVAL
Confetti Battle and Dancing
THURSDAY, AUGUST 7th

Rhayader & District Agricultural & Horticultural Show
THURSDAY, AUGUST 28th

ON EACH OF THE ABOVE DATES
CHEAP TICKETS will be issued to

RHAYADER

BY ANY ORDINARY TRAIN.

THURSDAY, AUGUST 7th.

FROM	Return Fares, Third Class.	Return Times, August 7th	FROM	Return Fares, Third Class.	Return Times, August 7th
	s. d.	p.m.		s. d.	p.m.
Builth Wells	1 9		St. Harmons	9	
Builth Road	1 6	5.50 8.54 or 10.0	Pantydwr	11	
Newbridge-on-Wye	1 0		Glan-yr-afon Halt	1 3	6.45, 7.45 or 10.0
Doldowlod	5		Tylwch	1 6	
			Llanidloes	1 9	

THURSDAY, AUGUST 28th.

FROM	Return Fares, Third Class.	Return Times, August 28th	FROM	Return Fares, Third Class.	Return Times, August 28th
	s. d.	p.m.		s. d.	p.m.
Brecon	5 6		St. Harmons	9	
Talyllyn	4 6		Pantydwr	11	
Talgarth	3 9	5.50	Glan-yr-afon Halt	1 3	6.45, 7.45 or 9.30
Three Cocks	3 0		Tylwch	1 6	
Boughrood & Llyswen	2 6		Llanidloes	1 9	
Erwood	2 3		Dolwen	2 6	
Aberedw			Llandinam	2 3	
Builth Wells	1 9		Moat Lane	2 9	
Builth Road	1 6	5.50 or 8.54	Newtown	3 6	6.45
Newbridge-on-Wye	1 0		Montgomery	4 3	
Doldowlod	5		Welshpool	5 0	

CONDITIONS OF ISSUE.

Children under Three years of age, Free; Three and under Fourteen, Half-price. Excursion and other tickets at fares less than the ordinary fares are issued subject to the Notices and Conditions shown in the Company's current Time Tables.

LUGGAGE ARRANGEMENTS.

CHEAP DAY TICKETS.—Passengers holding Cheap Day Tickets may carry with them 60lbs. of marketing goods at Owner's Risk, free of charge, all excess over that weight to be charged for. Passengers returning from Shopping Centres may take with them, free of charge, articles not exceeding in the aggregate 120lbs. (First Class) or 60lbs. (Third Class) which they have purchased for their own domestic use. Furniture, linoleum, musical instruments, cycles, mail carts, typewriters and other articles of a similar character are excepted from these arrangements.

Dogs accompanying Passengers are charged for at the single fare for the double journey, tickets available on day of issue only.

For any further information respecting the arrangements shown in this Bill, application should be made at any of the Company's Stations or Offices : to
Mr. H. WARWICK, District Traffic Manager, G.W.R. Oswestry : or to
Mr. D. V. NICHOLLS, ...

GREAT WESTERN RAILWAY.

Visit Barry Island, the Gem of the South Wales Seaside Resorts.

On SUNDAY, AUGUST 24th

HALF-DAY EXCURSION to

CARDIFF (QUEEN STREET)
AND
BARRY ISLAND

FROM	Leaving at	To Cardiff	To Barry Island
	a.m.	s. d.	d.
NEWTOWN	10 0	5 6	6 0
LLANIDLOES	10 20	5 6	6 0
RHAYADER	10 45	5 0	6 0
Newbridge-on-Wye	11 0	5 0	6 0
Builth Road	11 15	5 0	5 6
BUILTH WELLS	11 25	5 0	5 6
Erwood	11 35	4 6	5 0
Boughrood and Llyswen	11 40	4 6	5 0
Three Cocks	11 50	4 6	5 0
TALGARTH	11 45		
BRECON		4 0	4 6
Talyllyn	12 5 p.m.	4 0	4 6
Talybont-on-Usk	12 "	3 6	4 0
Pontsticill	12 50	2 6	3 0

| Cardiff (Queen Street) | arr. | 2 10 p.m. |
| Barry Island | arr. | 2 40 " |

Passengers return same day from Barry Island at 7.40 p.m., Cardiff (Queen Street) 8.5 p.m.

Note.—These Tickets will not be available for the Return Journey unless presented to and nipped by the Ticket Examiner on the Outward Journey.

TICKETS ISSUED AND DATED IN ADVANCE AT STATIONS AND OFFICES.

CONDITIONS OF ISSUE OF EXCURSION TICKETS AND OTHER REDUCED FARE TICKETS

Children under Three years of age, Free; Three and under Fourteen, Half-price. Excursion and other Tickets at fares less than the ordinary fares are issued subject to the Notices and Conditions shown in the Company's current Time Tables.

LUGGAGE ARRANGEMENTS.

DAY AND HALF-DAY EXCURSION TICKETS.—Passengers holding Day or Half-Day Excursion Tickets are not allowed to take any luggage except small handbags, luncheon baskets or other small articles intended for the passenger's use during the day. On the return journey only, passengers may take with them, free of charge, at Owner's Risk, goods for their own use, not exceeding in the aggregate 60lbs. Furniture, Linoleum, Musical Instruments, Cycles, Mail Carts, Typewriters and other articles of a similar character are excepted from these arrangements.

For any further information respecting the arrangements shown in this Bill, application should be made at any of the Company's Stations or Offices : :
Mr. H. WARWICK, District Traffic Manager, G.W.R. Oswestry; to
Mr. F. G. WAINWRIGHT, Divisional Superintendent, G.W.R. Cardiff; or to
Mr. R. H. NICHOLLS, Superintendent of the Line, Paddington Station. W

every day but only stopped on Friday to pick up for Brecon; the fifth stopped daily, the sixth stopped only on Wednesdays, the seventh stopped daily, the eighth ran only on Wednesdays, the ninth stopped each day, and the tenth was the only one that would not stop even on request to the guard!

Another problem the Great Western faced was that of motor buses. The Cambrian never had more than two, but the Great Western had jumped in heavily, starting in 1903 with a bus service in Cornwall, and extended to all parts of the system, with route buses and also excursion charabancs. Most other railways did the same, but on a much smaller scale than the GWR, and they more or less held the fields of their choice up to World War I. After that, the picture was different; there were ample supplies of ex-WD vehicles at prices a returning soldier could raise, and they began to run all over North Wales. The Great Western brought in a large number of modern buses, and these smart vehicles in brown and cream livery (and LMS-Crosvilles in LMS red) were a common sight for a few years. Then the 'Big Four' railways seem to have concluded that running motor buses was not really their business, and the routes and fleets were hived off to bus companies in which the railways held a major financial interest. The Great Western buses in the north part of the ex-Cambrian system were passed over to Western Transport, while those in the south part went to Western Welsh. The area through which the Mid-Wales Line passed had not developed many bus services; the only GWR depot was at Talgarth. However, in *Bradshaw* the Mid-Wales timetables had a note against Brecon: 'Station for Crickhowell; GWR buses meet principal trains; 80 minutes run'.

When bus and tram competition had begun soon after 1900, the railways had at first fought back by trying to turn some of their lines into bus routes by putting up halts served by frequent railcars or motor-trains. The Great Western and the London & South Western had led the way, though the Taff Vale Railway was also much in love with the railcar for many years. The Cambrian was not unaware, and drew up plans both for a self-contained steamcar and for a trailer to be worked by a light engine. However they did not proceed with either, building only one control car for running with a standard engine.

When the GWR took over, it was still in the full flush of halt-building, and peppered the Cambrian's coast line with them. On the Mid-Wales it was more difficult; a halt on a gradient of 1 in 60 would not be popular with drivers, and besides, almost every village down the line already had a station. A halt planned before the fusion was set up at Llangorse Lake, desirable because the walk to the lake from Talyllyn was difficult. Then one was added at Glan-yr-afon siding, and three halts were put up which were unashamedly for 'hikers': Marteg (1931), Llanstephan (1933) and Llanfaredd (1934). The term hiker was applied to country walkers at that time, which was enjoying an explosive boom; all the halts were short wooden affairs in delightful scenery. To alight at one, the passenger had to inform the guard at the previous stopping station. The word 'stopping' was necessary, because for example some trains missed out St Harmons, and it would be no good (assuming it was a corridor train) asking the guard at that point to stop the train at Marteg Halt.

Down Trains. MOAT LANE Jc., LLANIDLOES, BUILTH WELLS and BRECON. Week Days.

Miles from Moat Lane. M.C.	Miles from Whitchurch and M.P. Mileage M.C.	STATIONS.	Ruling Grad. direct 1 in	Passenger and Mail. B (SX) arr.	Passenger and Mail. B dep.	Passenger. B arr.	Passenger. B dep.	Pass. MO dep.	Passenger. B arr.	Passenger. B dep.	9.20 a.m. Hereford L.M.S. Passenger. arr.	9.20 a.m. dep.	Passenger. B arr.	Passenger. B dep.	Pass. MO dep.	Passenger. B arr.	Passenger. B dep.	2.55 Newport Pass. dep.	4.10 p.m. Hereford L.M.S. Passenger. arr.	4.10 p.m. dep.	Passenger. B arr.	Passenger. B dep.	6.46 p.m. N w port Pass. dep.	6.50 p.m. Whit-church Pass. arr.
	52 26	**MOAT LANE JCT.**	177 R.	a.m. T	a.m. 6 0	a.m.	a.m.	a.m.	a.m.	a.m.	a.m.	a.m.	p.m.	p.m.	p.m.	p.m.	p.m.	p.m.	p.m.	p.m.	p.m.	p.m.	p.m.	p.m.
2 7	54 33	Llandinam	225 R.		6 6					12 30				2 40			5 25						5 30	9 34
4 69	57 15	Dolwen	132 R.							12 35				2 46			5 30						5 36	9 40
7 57	59 76	**LLANIDLOES**	60 R.	6 16	6 19					12 41			2 51	2 53			5 41	5 45				5 41	5 45	9 45
10 69	63 15	Tylwch	77 R.		6 26									3 0				5 52						
12 39	64 65	Glan-yr-afon Halt	80 F.	6 34 Z									3 9 X	3 4				5 56						
14 63	67 9	Pant-y-dwr												3 12				6 1						
16 11	68 37	St. Harmons											3 16				6 6							
18 70	71 16	Marteg Halt											3 21				6 12½							
21 40	73 66	Rhayader	70 F.	6 47	X6 49						3 28	3 32			6 19	6 20								
24 62	77 8	Doldowlod	60 F.		6 55							3 30			6 27	X6 35								
28 69	81 15	Newbridge-on-Wye	75 R/F.		7 1		9 52				3 49			6 41										
32 66	85 12	Builth Road	75 F.	7 12	7 17	9 13		10 3			3 56	3 57		6 50	6 54			5 13			7 28			
34 33	86 59	**BUILTH WELLS**	100 F.	7 20			10 15		12 46	B		4 0	4 1		6 54		5 15	5 20	5 22		5 35	5 38	9 51	9 57
36 27	88 53	Llanfaredd Halt		9 10	10 32					4 12½								5 27×	5W29						
38 35	90 61	Aberedw	74 R.	B 9 15	10 3					4 19														
41 15	93 41	Erwood	75 R.	9 19½				B			4 23			7 9											
43 38	95 64	Llanstephan Halt	75 F.	9 24						4 29			7 13												
45 34	97 60	Boughrood & Llyswen	75 R.	9 30						4 33½			7 17												
48 18	100 44	Three Cocks	75 F.	9 40 X9 41	10 34		8.3 a.m. Newport Passenger.		1 T35		4 38½			7 23											
49 69	102 15	Talgarth	75 R.	9 46	8 5	9 52	a.m.	10 29	10 33	1 42		4 45	4 46		7 29		5 13	5 20							
53 9	105 27	Trefeinon	75 R.	X9 58	8 11		a.m. dep. 10 40	10 38	X1042	1 48			4 53		7 35		5 27×								
55 27	107 9	Llangorse Lake Halt		10 2	8 18		10 45	10 48	X1051	1 56		S			7 42										
55 52	107 78	Talyllyn Junction N.		V			a.m. 10 34	10x57	11T 2	1 57					7 47										
56 17	108 29	Talyllyn	75 R.	8X25	8T27	5 10 7	10 49	10X40	10x57	11T 2	2 4 X2 11	4T58	5 0		7 50	7 53	9T14	U	10110					
58 5	5	Groesffordd Halt	350 R.	8 36	8 32	10 15	10X49	10 45	11 10	2 20	2 16	5 71 x	5 28	5 46	8 2	9 12	10 18							
59 —	71	**BRECON**																						

Notes within table: "Arrives Talyllyn 5.10 p.m."

STANDARD LOADS OF PASSENGER, ETC., TRAINS—continued.

CLASS OF ENGINE.

SECTION. From	To	29XX; 43, 53, 63, 73, 78, 83 and 93XX; 31, 41, 51, 61 and 81XX; 58 and 66XX.	3300, 3455; 4400-4410; 4500-4599; 5500-5574; 36, 37, 52, 77, 87, and 97XX. 0-6-2 T. "B" Group.	3200, 3219; 3252-3291; 2251-2299. 0-6-2 T. "A" Group.	0-6-0 and 0-6-0 T.	2-4-0 T. Metro. 0-4-2 T. 48 and 58XX; 898, 900.	0-4-2 T. 517 Class. 1334, 1335, 1336.
		Tons.	Tons.	Tons.	Tons.	Tons.	Tons.
Brecon	Builth Wells	—	—	—	192	168	
Builth Wells	Llanidloes	—	—	336	192	144	
Llanidloes	Moat Lane Junction	—	—		312	264	

BRECON AND MOAT LANE JUNCTION.

From	To	Tons.	Tons.	Tons.	Tons.	Tons.	Tons.
Moat Lane Junction	Llanidloes	—	—	308	288	216	216
Llanidloes	Talyllyn Junction	—	—	*	192	168	168
Talyllyn Junction	Brecon				192		

Up Trains. BRECON, BUILTH WELLS, LLANIDLOES and MOAT LANE Jc. Week Days.

Y—Calls at Llangorse Lake Halt on first and third Tuesdays in the month. (Not advertised.) W—Sets down passengers on Wednesdays only. Y—Does not run when Brecon County School is closed.
Z—Calls to set down passengers on notice to guard, or to pick up passengers when signalled to do so. ¶—Calls to set down passengers on notice to the guard.

STATIONS	L.M.S. Passenger to Hereford (G) arr	dep	L.E. SXR (G) dep	Passenger (B) arr	dep	Pass. to Merthyr (B) dep	Pass. MO (B) dep	Passenger (B) arr	dep	L.M.S. Passenger to Hereford (B) arr	dep	Passenger to Newport (B) arr	dep	Passenger to Newport MO (B) arr	dep	Passenger SX (B) arr	dep	Passenger and Mail (B) arr	dep	L.M.S. Pass. to Hereford (B) dep	Pass. to Newport (B) dep	Passenger SO (B) arr	dep
	a.m.	a.m.	a.m.	a.m.	a.m.	a.m.	a.m.	a.m.	a.m.	a.m.	a.m.	p.m.	p.m.	p.m.	p.m.	p.m.	p.m.	p.m.	p.m.	p.m.	p.m.	p.m.	p.m.
BRECON	—	6 50	—	—	7 15	—	—	—	10 30	—	10 51	—	12 5	—	—	—	4 10	—	5§11	5 58	6 10	—	X9 20
Groesffordd Halt	6 58	6 59			7 23				10 35		10 59	12 10	12 18			4 15	4 20		X5 22	X6 18	6 15		X9 25
Talyllyn			7 33		7 37	7 45	9 35	10 39	10 43			12 14	12 18		2 9	4 19			5 18½	6 25	X6 21	9 24	9 30
Talyllyn Junction North					7 41	7 50	9 30		10X43						X2 16		4 24		X5 22				9 37
Llangorse Lake Halt						7 56	9 46										4 28		5 30				
Trefeinon	7 6	7 13		7 37	7 47			10 46	10X50	11 2	11 9					4 33	4 34		5 35			9 28	9 37
Talgarth	7 11	7 18		7 41	7 53			10 55	10 57	11 7	11 13					4 39	4 44		5 41	5 42		9 30	9 40
Three Cocks	7 18	7 20	7 55	7 46	7 57			11 1	11 9	11 11	11 18						4 50			5 48		9 44	9 55
Boughrood and Llyswen				7 53	8 9				11 13½								4 51		5 52½				10 1
Llanstephan Halt				8 7½	8 14				11 20								5 5		5 59				10 7
Erwood				8 14	8 20				11 26								5 11½		6 5				10 12
Aberedw				8 20	8 26				11 31														10 18
Llanfaredd Halt				8 26	8 34																		
BUILTH WELLS	8T18	8 23		8 34½	8 42	8 55		11 25		12 53	12 50	1 19	1 12	2 48	2 45	5 15		6 12	6 15		10 25		
Builth Road	8 23			8 42	8 50	8 58					12 54		X11 21	2 57	2 49			6 18	6 19	6 35			
Newbridge-on-Wye					8 56								1 27½							6 27			
Doldowlod					9 12½														Y6 50	6 43	X6 36		
Rhayader	8 49				9 25						1 39		Z					Z 2			6 44		
Marteg Halt																				Y 7			
St. Harmons																			7 10	7 18	T7 12		
Pantydwr											1 43½								7 18		X7 21		
Glan-yr-afon Halt								11 25		1 54	1 48					1 54							
Tylwch	6 40	7 35		9 12½				11 30			1 55					2 0			7 31	7 31	T7 26		
LLANIDLOES	6 45	7 40		9T22	9 25			11 35			2 0					2 5			7 37	7 37	T7 33		
Dolwen	6 50	7 45			9 35																		
Llandinam		7 46						11 40		2 10													
MOAT LANE JUNCTION	6 54	7 50		9 39																			

R—Does not run when Brecon County School is closed. S—Calls on Saturdays only. Y—Calls on Wednesdays and Saturdays only.
W—Calls on Wednesdays only. Z—Calls to set down passengers on notice to guard, or to pick up passengers when signalled to do so.
‡—Arrives two minutes earlier. §—Advertised one minute earlier. ¶—Arrives one minute earlier.

List of Signal Boxes—continued.

Distance between Signal Boxes. (M. C.)	NAME OF BOX.	Week Days Opened. Mondays.	Week Days Opened. Other Days.	Closed at.	Sundays Opened at.	Sundays Closed at.	Whether provided with Switch.
	MOAT LANE AND BRECON SECTION.						
7 41¾	Llanidloes	3.30 a.m.	2.10 a.m.	11.40 p.m.	2.10 a.m.	8.25 a.m.	—
3 27½	Tylwch†	—	—	—		Closed	Yes.
3 76½	Pantydwr	4. 0 a.m.		8.30 p.m. 8X		8. 0 a.m.	—
		10.30 p.m.	10.30 p.m.	—...	—		
6 58	Rhayader	4.30 a.m.	—	8.45 p.m. 8X	—		—
		11. 0 p.m.	11. 0 p.m.			7.30 a.m.	
3 23	Doldowlod	4.50 a.m.		8.55 p.m. 8X	—		—
		11.40 p.m.	11.40 p.m.	10. 5 p.m. 8O		7. 0 a.m.	
4 4	Newbridge-on-Wye	5. 0 a.m.		9. 5 p.m. 8X	—		—
		11.50 p.m.	11.50 p.m.	9.55 p.m. 8O		6.35 a.m.	
3 66	Builth Road	5.10 a.m.	12. 5 a.m.	9,10 p.m. 8X	12. 5 a.m.	.6.25 a.m.	—
				9.40 p.m. 8O			
1 40	Builth Wells	4. 0 a.m.	—		—	8. 0 a.m.	—
6 66	Erwood	5.20 a.m.	5.20 a.m.	6.15 p.m.	Closed		Yes.
4 18	Boughrood and Llyswen	5.20 a.m.	5.20 a.m.	6.15 p.m.	Closed		Yes.
2 66	Three Cocks Junction	5.20 a.m.	5.20 a.m.	10. 0 p.m. 8X	Closed		—
				10.35 p.m. 8O			
2 32	Talgarth	5.45 a.m.	5.45 a.m.	10.10 p.m.	Closed		Yes.
2 84	Trefeinon	6.40 a.m.	6.40 a.m.	11.15 a.m.	Closed		Yes.
		1.15 p.m.	1.15 p.m.	6. 0 p.m.	Closed		
2 49	Talyllyn Junction North	5.45 a.m.	5.45 a.m.	10.20 p.m.	Closed		—
— 33	Talyllyn Junction West	5.40 a.m.	5.40 a.m.	10.25 p.m.	Closed		—
3 71	Brecon	5.20 a.m.	5.20 a.m.	10.35 p.m.	Closed		—

†—Opens as instructed by District Inspector.

Speed Restrictions—continued.

DOWN LINE.

The speed of any train between Moat Lane Junction and Brecon must not exceed 40 miles per hour, and must be further restricted to lower speeds as shewn below:

Moat Lane Junction Y	Main Line	..	Branch	10
Llanidloes Y	Any Train through Station	..	..	15
Llanidloes and Tylwch	61 m. 30 ch.	.. (Over Curves).	61 m. 40 ch.	30
Llanidloes and Tylwch	61 m. 65 ch.	.. (Over Curves).	62 m. 25 ch.	15
Llanidloes and Tylwch	62 m. 60 ch.	.. (Over Curves).	63 m. 0 ch.	30
Tylwch	Any Train through Station	..		10
Tylwch and Pantydwr	63 m. 50 ch.	.. (Over Curves).	64 m. 10 ch.	30
Tylwch and Pantydwr	64 m. 45 ch.	.. (Over Curves).	65 m. 40 ch.	20
Pantydwr	Any Train through Station	..		10
*St. Harmons and Rhayader	70 m. 10 ch.	.. (Over Curves).	70 m. 55 ch.	15
St. Harmons and Rhayader	71 m. 5 ch.	.. (Over Curves).	71 m. 65 ch.	15
Rhayader	Any Train through Station	..		10
Doldowlod	Any Train through Station	..		10
Newbridge-on-Wye	Any Train through Station	..		10
Builth Road	Any Train through Station	..		15
Builth Wells	Any Train through Station	..		15
Aberedw and Erwood	90 m. 50 ch.	.. (Over Curves).	91 m. 20 ch.	30
Erwood Z	Any Train through Station	..		10
*Erwood and Boughrood	94 m. 60 ch.	.. (Over Curves).	95 m.p.	25
Boughrood	Any Train through Station	..		10
Three Cocks	Any Train through Station	..		10
Three Cocks Junction	L.M.S. Line	..	Main Line	10
Three Cocks and Talgarth	101 m. 50 ch.	.. (Over Curves).	102 m. 70 ch.	30
Talgarth	Any Train through Station	..		10
Talgarth and Trefeinon	103 m. 20 ch.	.. (Over Curves).	105 m. 20 ch.	30
Trefeinon Z	Any Train through Station	..		15
Trefeinon and Talyllyn	105 m. 73 ch.	..	107 m. 66 ch.	30
Talyllyn North Junction	Any Train through Junction	..		10
Talyllyn West Junction	Any Train through Junction	..		10
Talyllyn	4 m. 5 ch.	..	3 m. 70 ch.	10
Brecon Yard Ground Frame	—		—	20
Brecon Yard	Any Engine and Goods Train	over Straight Siding	..	5
Brecon Station	Facing connections	..	Loop	15

*—Permanent Speed Restriction Indicator provided.
§—Drivers to keep a sharp look-out for hand signals from Watchmen at Harlech Cliff and Frog Cutting.
R— See note on page 22.
Y—The speed of any train worked by an engine in the " Yellow " classification must not exceed 15 m.p.h. when passing over the Severn River Bridge at 58 m. 36¾ ch.
Z—This restriction applies only when the Signal Box is open. When it is closed trains may travel at ordinary speed.

Extract from the Great Western Working Timetable, October 1942

On 31st December, 1930 the ex-Midland Railway trains from Hereford ceased to run beyond Brecon. The Great Western Railway therefore on 1st January, 1931 put on a service from Brecon to Neath (Riverside). It is rather surprising to realise that it was some 40 years since any train on the former Neath & Brecon Railway had run between those two towns. The Great Western had never shown any interest in Brecon, though it had owned the Brecknock & Abergavenny Canal since 1880.

During the 'thirties the Great Western made great efforts to stimulate traffic on the Mid-Wales line by excursions and cheap tickets. Such events as the Brecon Agricultural Show, the Radnorshire Show, or the Shrewsbury Floral Fête were the occasion for cheap fares or special trains, though timetabled trains were more often used. There were some remarkable long-distance excursions, such as Builth Wells to Liverpool, good value at 6s. (30p). Another 6s. 'snip' was an excursion from Llanidloes to Barry Island on a Sunday. Bearing in mind that the rolling stock used was not of the best, some of them must have been a bit exhausting: for example, from Llanidloes to Weston-super-Mare, 5 hours 52 minutes for 10s. 6d. (52½p). It started at 5.20 am and by midnight the return train had not even got as far as Newport! Passengers on these trains could not take any luggage, but could bring back articles up to 60 lb. weight, provided it was 'not a musical instrument, mail cart, typewriter, or article of a similar character' — not that there would have been anyone around to check when the travellers from Weston-super-Mare staggered off the train at 3 am.

Another interesting feature of the immediate pre-War years was a train which possibly took the title of the longest 'all-stations' journey. It was from Neath to Whitchurch via Brecon, Moat Lane, and Oswestry, 145 miles. It involved 54 stops and four more conditional ones. Engines were changed at Brecon; the average speed was just over 20 mph which is not too bad for such a train.

Goods traffic on the line had always been varied. Although timber had been handled at two of the private sidings and stone at the Llanelwedd siding, there were no important industries; it was through traffic, apart from some local sheep transfers. A foreman on the line from 1920 to 1964, Gareth Morgan, recalled some of what went through. There was slate from the Cambrian's northern lines going to South Wales; dolomite from the Llynclys quarry to Ebbw Vale and Dowlais (one train per day for many years). Some structural steel, fabricated or semi-fabricated, came off the Cheshire Lines Railway and down through the Mid-Wales for export at Cardiff.

However, a greater impression was made on him by the excursion traffic; he recalled miners coming from Treherbert with bags of coal which they exchanged in Aberystwyth for bags of potatoes. In the mid-'twenties a train from Barry to Llandrindod Wells via the Builth Road loop actually had a dining car. As a junior porter he had seen the 'Jellicoe Specials' passing, and of course coal formed a good part of the goods traffic as on all lines, but the huge stacks in the yards awaiting the pleasure of large house owners were absent, because so much wood was available for domestic fires. However, towns like Rhayader and Newbridge with their many boarding houses did need a lot of coal in the summer to keep the kitchen range turning out meals.

Altogether, the Mid-Wales was a good example of the way in which for so many decades the railways carried everything; the only trouble was that in such an unpopulated countryside there was never quite enough to carry for the line to be profitable.

There was always an unfavourable comparison to be made between the Mid-Wales line and the Central Wales line in terms of through carriage availability. On the latter even in the winter timetables up to the 1939 War there was at Builth Road a morning through coach to Euston, a mid-day one to Liverpool with restaurant car attached, an afternoon one to Manchester and a late evening one to York. It would have been pointless for the Great Western to try to compete; it could only pocket a few bob from people holidaying at Newbridge or Builth Wells who used its trains to reach those sleek red vehicles at Builth Road.

The '2301' class engines dominated the scene, but occasional visitors to the Mid-Wales line had been the small 0−4−2T engines so common on the rest of the GWR: in 1933 a modern version of these was produced, the '48XX' class, and these were noted at times from 1935 on Mid-Wales trains. Another visitor was the light 0−6−0 pannier tank, a rebuild of an early class of 0−6−0ST, which was sometimes seen at Builth Wells, though more often at Oswestry. These were allowed on the Mid-Wales, while the other classes of 0−6−0PT transferred to the Cambrian were not, nor were the Collett '2201' class 0−6−0s which were appearing further north.

A train which intrigued enthusiasts in the late 'thirties was that mentioned above from Barry to Llandrindod Wells, the only regular service to use the Builth Road spur. Their interest came from the fact that the train had to be propelled along the spur in both directions, and as there was no turntable at Llandrindod Wells the engine had to work tender-first back to Builth Road. Here the return train met a local from Builth Wells, which was hauled by a Cardiff engine also running tender-first, and the two trains exchanged engines to put things right. Not much stop-watch work was done on the Mid-Wales, but one magazine correspondent who did the Llandrindod Wells trip described his return, in three coaches with a '2301' 0−6−0, logging a start-to-stop speed to Talgarth of 40 mph 'and all but 60 mph between Phillips Siding and Boughrood'.

The end of through Midland services to Swansea brought some changes to locomotives on the Three Cocks to Brecon section; the old Johnson 0−4−4Ts gave way to ex-LNWR 2−4−2Ts, and by 1938 to ex-L&YR 0−6−0s.

The late 'thirties were the best years the Cambrian ever had for holiday traffic. The Mid-Wales had some share; a surprising amount of red livery was noted, with spare LMS coaches sometimes parked at Moat Lane. But then came World War II. Once again some of the Dean 0−6−0s were impressed by the Army; No. 2447 was one of those on the Mid-Wales which received a sudden call. This time also not all returned, some being captured at the time of Dunkirk and ending up in various odd corners of Europe. This time there were no coal trains from the south to keep the line busy, and the War years were very quiet. On one occasion an ex-Midland Railway '2F' 0−6−0 was noted on the line, and there were probably other visitors, but nobody around to note them.

Chapter Nine
Nationalisation

Nationalisation in 1948 brought little change other than some dropping-off of goods traffic through Talyllyn from the former Midland, now that the routes were no longer in competition. A big event in the Claerwen Valley on 22nd October, 1952, the opening of the largest of all the dams, sadly brought no joy to the Mid-Wales line; the authorities were doubtful of the wisdom of sending the Royal Train over the viaducts on that line and brought it instead to Llandrindod Wells, whence the party went by road to Rhayader. Though the Birmingham Corporation had intended to relay the Elan branch for future dam work, when the time came the development of off-the-road vehicles had made it unnecessary.

The timetables remained very much the same. There were now 24 trains per day passing between Talyllyn and Brecon, counting both directions: eight ex-Midland, eight ex-Brecon & Merthyr and eight ex-Cambrian; of the northbound Mid-Wales trains, two went through to Moat Lane, one provided a connection to Moat Lane at Builth Road, and one terminated at Builth with no connection. The extension platform at Brecon was still sometimes used, a Hereford train running through the main platform to allow a Merthyr train to come in behind.

When shed numbers were allocated in 1950, and carried on small plates on smoke-box doors, Llanidloes and Moat Lane were given 89A, and Builth Wells and Brecon 89B, all sub-sheds of Oswestry. Builth Road became a Shrewsbury sub-shed, 86G. These were altered later; in 1959 Brecon became 89A, and in 1961 Oswestry became a sub-shed of Shrewsbury. Brecon was now 88K (sub to Cardiff Valleys) and Builth Road 84G; Builth Wells shed was closed by this time, having gone in September 1957; the two class '2' 2−6−0 engines there were transferred to Builth Road.

The appearance of the class '2' 'LMS-type' moguls on the line signalled the progressive withdrawal of the '2301s'. Just before nationalisation Hawksworth on the GWR had plans drawn up for a light 0−6−0 to take their place, in view of the fact that the Collett 0−6−0s were too heavy for the line. After 1948 this was not proceeded with, but some tests on 'Great Westernising' the standard light moguls on the LMS, being continued by British Railways as the standard '2P', showed that this type could give roughly the same performance as a '2301'. The latter did not fade away quickly; it was seven years after the first trial runs of the moguls that the last '2301' class went.

Three of these engines remained in 1955; Nos. 2516, 2538 and 2301. The last two had been sharing a working comprising a thrice-weekly pick-up goods from Oswestry to Newtown, a trip up the Kerry branch (which was closed in May 1956), a run light to Moat Lane, and then the evening train to Brecon, working back the next day. All three were now enthusiasts' pets, and No. 2538 was selected to assist a Society run to Towyn in September 1956. No. 2301 was withdrawn, and then No. 2516 was chosen for preservation and left for Swindon, where it is now displayed in the Railway Museum there. No. 2538 soldiered on, being noted on Brecon workings on several occasions — a prime catch for a photographer, being the last of a

Table 185—*continued*

BRECON, HEREFORD, BUILTH ROAD, LLANIDLOES and MOAT LANE

WEEK DAYS ONLY

Miles		am	am	am	am	am	am	am	am	am	am	am	pm	pm	pm	pm	pm	pm	pm	pm	pm	pm	pm	pm	pm	pm
	Brecon dep					6 50	7 35		8 15		1025		1210		1 20			2 5	4 10	5 5	6 0	6 0		6 15	8 15	9 35
2	Groesffordd Halt						7 40		8 20		1030		1215		1 25			2 10	4 15	5 10	6 4			6 20		9 41
4	Talyllyn Junction arr					6 59	7 45		8 25		1035		1220		1 30			2 15	4 20	5 15	6 9	6 8		6 25	8 23	9 46
—	121 Cardiff D 131 dep						To Newport (Table 121)				8 15		To Newport (Table 121)		10a58			To Newport (Table 121)		2S38				To Newport (Table 121)		6 55
—	121 Newport „										8 3				11a15					3S 0						7 7
—	Talyllyn Junction dep					7 0			8 30		1040				1 33				4 21	5C17	6 10	6 9			Saturdays only	9 47
5½	Llangorse Lake Halt					dd			8 33		1044				1 37				4 24	dd	6 14	6 14				9 53
7	Trefeinon Halt					7 9			8 38		1050				1 42				4 30	dd		dd				9 59
9½	Talgarth					7 15			8 44		1055				1 48				4 36	5C32	6 23	6 23				10 6
11¾	**Three Cocks Junction** arr					**7 21**			**8 50**		**11 2**				**1 55**				**4 45**	**5C38**	**6 29**	**6 29**				**1012**
	Three Cocks Junction dep					**7 22**			**8 51**		**11 6**	**1115**			**1 59**	**2 15**			**4 49**	**5 40**		**6 30**				**1020**
13½	Glasbury-on-Wye					7 26					11 9					2 19			4 53		Except Saturdays	6 34		Saturdays only	To Bargoed (Table 121)	Saturdays only
17½	**Hay-on-Wye**					**7 36**					**1119**					**2 29**			**5 2**			**6 44**				
21	Whitney-on-Wye					7 44					1128					2 37			5 11			6 53				
24½	Eardisley					7 51					1136					2 44			5 18			7 1				
26	Kinnersley					7 56					1141					2 49			5 23							
29½	Moorhampton					8 3					1148					2 57										
32½	Credenhill					bb					1159					3 8										
38½	**Hereford** arr					**8 28**					**1216**					**3 24**			**5 59**			**7 40**				
14¾	Boughrood and Llyswen								8 56			1120			2 4				Except Saturdays	5 46		Saturdays only			Commences 11th May, 1963	1027
16½	Llanstephan Halt								9 0			1126			2 11					dd						1032
18¾	Erwood								9 7			1140			2 17					5 57						1040
21¼	Aberedw								dd			1148			2 24					dd						1045
23¼	Llanfaredd Halt								dd			dd			2 28		Except Saturdays and School Holidays									
25¼	**Builth Wells** arr								**9 22**			**1158**			**2 32**					**6 13**						**1055**
	Builth Wells dep				**7 45**			9 0	**9 30**			**12 5**		**1245**	**2 36**					**6 20**			7 50			
27½	**Builth Road** arr				**7 49**			9 3	**9 33**			**12 9**		**1249**	**2 42**					**6 24**			7 54			
	(Low Level) dep				**7 50**									**1250**	**2 48**					**6 26**						
31	Newbridge-on-Wye F				7 58									1258	2 55					6 38						
35¼	Doldowlod Halt				8 5									1 6	3 2					dd						
38¼	Rhayader				8 13									1 15	3 10					6 54						
41	Marteg Halt				8 20									1 21	dd											
43¾	St. Harmons				8 29									1 30	3 24					7 6						
45¼	Pantydwr				8 32									1 33	3 28					7 10						
47¼	Glan-yr-afon Halt				8 39									1 38	dd					dd						
49	Tylwch Halt				8 43									1 42	3 37					dd						
52¼	**Llanidloes** arr				**8 51**									**1 50**	**3 46**					**7 27**						
	Llanidloes dep	**6 15**	**7 10**	**8 5**	**8 55**					**11 5**				**1 54**	**3 47**		**4 15**			**7 30**						
55	Dolwen Halt	6 20	7 15	8 10	9 1					11 10				1 59	dd		4 19			dd						
58	Llandinam	6 25	7 21	8 15	9 6					11 15				2 5	3 58		4 25			7 40						
60	**Moat Lane Junction** arr	**6 30**	**7 27**	**8 20**	**9 12**					**11 21**				**2 10**	**4 3**		**4 31**			**7 45**						
103½	184 Aberystwyth arr				1142					2 10				5 13			7 25			9 30						
78½	184 Welshpool „	7 4	8 8		9 55					12 6				2 53	5 22		5 22			8 35						
112¼	184 Whitchurch „	8 58			1212					2 25				4 29	7S51					10 8						

a am
bb Calls to set down on notice to the Guard at Moorhampton and to take up on notice to the Station Master at Credenhill

C On Sats. dep Talyllyn Jn. 5 21 pm, Talgarth 5 34 and arr Three Cocks Jn. 5 41 pm
D Queen Street, via Bargoed

dd Calls if required on notice to Guard at previous stopping station or by giving hand-signal during daylight only

F 4¼ miles to Llandrindod Wells Station
S Saturdays only

British Railways (Western Region) 1962 Public timetable

Table 185

MOAT LANE, LLANIDLOES, BUILTH ROAD, HEREFORD and BRECON
WEEK DAYS ONLY

Miles	Station			
	184 Whitchurch .... dep			
	184 Welshpool .... "			
	184 Aberystwyth .... dep			
2	Moat Lane Junction .... dep			
2	Llandinam			
5	Dolwen Halt			
7½	Llanidloes .... arr / dep			
11	Tylwch Halt			
12½	Glan-yr-afon Halt			
14½	Pantydwr			
16½	St. Harmons			
19	Marteg Halt			
22½	Rhayader			
24½	Doldowlod Halt			
29	Newbridge-on-Wye F			
32	Builth Road (Low Level) .... arr / dep			
34½	Builth Wells			
36	Llanfaredd Halt			
38½	Aberedw			
41	Erwood			
43	Llanstephan Halt			
45	Boughrood and Llyswen			
	Mls Hereford .... dep			
5	Credenhill			
9½	Moorhampton			
12½	Kinnersley			
14½	Eardisley			
17½	Whitney-on-Wye			
21½	Hay-on-Wye			
25½	Glasbury-on-Wye			
48½	Three Cocks Junction .... arr / dep			
50½	Talgarth			
53	Trefeinon Halt			
54½	Llangorse Lake Halt			
56	Talyllyn Junction .... arr			
98½	121 Newport .... arr			
96½	121 Cardiff D 131 .... "			
	Talyllyn Junction .... dep			
58	Groesffordd Halt			
60	Brecon .... arr			

Footnotes:

aa Calls to take up on notice being given to the Station Master at Talgarth. Passengers wishing to alight must give notice to Guard at Talgarth

D Queen Street, via Bargoed

dd Calls if required on notice to Guard at previous stopping station or by giving hand signal during daylight only

F 4½ miles to Llandrindod Wells Station

c On Saturdays arr 3 6 pm

P 4 minutes later on Saturdays

s Saturdays only

uu Calls to set down on notice being given to Guard at previous stopping station

X Except Saturdays and School Holidays

class first built nearly 70 years previously. However on 20th May, 1957 this grand old lady was summoned to Swindon to be looked over, and the decision was taken to withdraw her. The Mid-Wales line would never be the same (it only had five more years of life anyway); though the '2301' class had many associations, including its WD work, its closest was with the Mid-Wales, for the rest of the Cambrian had had a multitude of GWR classes, but apart from the few remaining ex-Cambrian 0−6−0s, the Mid-Wales really only had one engine class after 1922.

The last original Cambrian engine had gone in 1954; the company had ordered four new class '89' 0−6−0s from Beyer Peacock after the War, which arrived in 1918/19. GW No. 873 was destroyed when it was thrown off Friog Rocks near Fairbourne in 1933, but the others worked on until 1953/4. They were officially banned from the Mid-Wales lines, but No. 873 was noted at Hereford in 1953; it could of course have got there via Shrewsbury.

There was some new traffic between Talyllyn and Three Cocks from 1958; the closing of the line from Dowlais via Brynmawr to Abergavenny Junction forced a regular service of ammonia tankers from Dowlais to Durham to travel over the Mid-Wales and Hereford lines; standard pannier tanks worked the trains — these were allowed on the Mid-Wales south of Three Cocks. Two of them were noted struggling up Torpantau bank towards Talyllyn with 36 tank wagons on one occasion.

Another short-lived traffic was that of National Service men to and from the Sennybridge Camp on the former Neath & Brecon line, most of whom came via Hereford. Two Collett 0−6−0s were seen on a ten-coach train of ex-LNER stock. However, on 11th November, 1961 the long shadow of Beeching began to fall, when the last train from Merthyr to Pontsticill Junction (former Brecon & Merthyr Railway) ran.

An up goods train entering Builth Road in September 1949 hauled by a Dean Goods 0−6−0 No. 2516.   *T.J. Edgington*

Chapter Ten

The Line Closes

Details emerged in early Spring of 1962 of proposals to be put to the Transport Users' Consultative Committee to close all the three lines into Brecon. Opposition began to swell from local, county and national levels. It was especially bitter for the town of Brecon; it had lost the former Neath & Brecon goods station at Ely Place in 1955, and now it was to be without any rail contact. Memoranda from all interested parties were forwarded to the Committee, but they did not make very encouraging reading. There were plenty of criticisms of past service, especially bad connections, and accusations of feeble management, tempered by praise for the local staffs. One councillor stated that if he wished to be in Cardiff for lunch, he had to take the 6.15 am from Llanidloes and travel via Gobowen, Shrewsbury and Hereford; in fact one of the most sensible suggestions made was that the early train from Moat Lane, leaving at 5.45 am, should be 'expedited' to Builth Road, to connect there with the 6.30 am departure, which had a connection to Cardiff arriving at 10.47. It certainly was very annoying that the early train should arrive at Builth only 37 minutes after the southbound train had left; but the 5.45 had connections all the way back to Whitchurch and would be difficult to 'expedite'.

The Montgomeryshire County Council produced the lofty statement that 'financial gain was not the first or even the main consideration'. The idea that British Rail was hoping to reduce its losses on such services deserved a less prissy response. Brecon Borough Council pointed out that there had been no change in the working of the Hereford line since it opened a century earlier, and this was largely true. Newtown Council strongly attacked the withdrawal of through trains to and from South Wales. Amongst the laments of Llanidloes Council was that while at one time goods handed in at Liverpool before 5 pm had been in Llanidloes by 9 am the next day, now it took 10–14 days!

It was clear however, that many of the objectors had grasped the important point, that it was a through line that was being scrapped, not some branch that had only local importance. One suggestion was that the 9.55 am from Moat Lane should be 'dieselised', stop at fewer stations, pick up and set down Brecon passengers at Talyllyn or Talgarth, and run through over the former B&M to Cardiff or Newport; a return train would pick up passengers off the 5.17 pm from Brecon at Talyllyn and be back at Moat Lane by 7.45 pm. The 9.55 train was booked to stop at all 25 stations to Brecon, including all halts, taking 2 hours 40 minutes. This disgraceful example should surely have made British Rail look at what could be done by scrapping many stations, as was done on a number of lines, to give better through connections. But it seems the authorities were already savouring the delights of closing three lines at once, and were deaf to such suggestions.

Not surprisingly, the proposals went through; the Neath & Brecon line was the first to close, on 15th October, 1962. On 30th December the Stephenson Locomotive Society ran an outing from Shrewsbury via the Mid-Wales to Brecon, and back via Three Cocks and Hereford, to give members a last taste of two lines at least. On the next day the last train ran, well-filled, with its almost obligatory centenarian. His memories of the early days were not recorded by the Press. They probably did not miss much; one local man informed the author that all Mid-Wales trains had been fitted with cow-catchers.

Apart from the general public, other losers were the Co-operative Wholesale Society, who had made regular use of their siding at Builth Wells, and Amalgamated Roadstone, who lost the Llanelwedd quarry siding. However, Rhayader yard was left open for coal concentration (not rail connected) until 5th April, 1965, as were the depots at Builth Wells and Talgarth. A freight-only connection to Neath was worked until 4th May, 1964. The part of the line which had originally been L&N remained open for freight until 2nd October, 1967. This was mainly to serve work on the Clwedog hydro-electric station then being completed. Dolwen station was closed entirely, but Llandinam remained open for full-load goods, as did Llanidloes.

Replacement bus services got off to a poor start and soon dwindled. The area south of Llanidloes has shown little development compared with other parts of Wales; the sparse service now operated on the Central Wales line is an indication of how low is the expectation of public transport in these parts. However, the Mid-Wales line had an importance that the Central Wales did not share; it was a way of going from North to South Wales without doing so through England, something common with the equally-closed former Manchester & Milford. One cannot help feeling that had the sense of Welsh nationality been as developed 20 years ago as it is now, public opinion would have insisted that it retained its own north to south route. Which would it have been? Both had fierce gradients and dubious

Builth Wells station around 1960 looking in the down direction with No. 46503 passing through. The Mid-Wales locomotive shed and carriage repair shop were situated on the right.
Oakwood Press

bridges, but the M&M route had the disadvantages of a reversal at Aberystwyth and the fact that Carmarthen was still a long way from Newport or Cardiff. At any rate, any motorist railway-lover glimpsing the imposing embankment on the other side of the Wye as he drives up through Rhayader must regret that so much splendid engineering has gone to waste, and as a taxpayer would surely not have grudged a few more thousands on the rural lines' subsidy to be able to travel an all-Welsh north to south route, as dreamed of from 1845 on, and now gone after a century of service.

Much of the Mid-Wales Railway's trackbed has gone back to farming, but a good deal lies in worthless land where the effort of making it good is not economic. The girders of the high river bridges were removed but the piers stand. Some smaller bridges have proved useful; the two north of the Marteg tunnel have recently been redecked for a farm track.

Many structures too have been put to use; the station building at Twlych has made an excellent house, named 'Twlych Halt'. At Rhayader the buildings are now serving as offices and stores for the local council engineers; Erwood station is a gift-shop with railway memorabilia on sale. At Three Cocks a Calorgas depot has been set up and a concrete memorial placed giving the date of closure of the station.

Wild-life has also benefited; apart from having some valuable wild habitat gifted to it, Marteg tunnel is the home to a breed of rare bats.

Doldowlod has been turned into a caravan site, with nameboards on display and home and distant signals at the gate. These unfortunately are not from the line; they are said to have come from Montgomery.

A train from Brecon to Moat Lane, hauled by class '2', 2−6−0 No. 46520 stands outside the Talyllyn West Junction signal box awaiting the right of way.

Oakwood Press

Appendix

Extracts from 1921 Appendix to the Rule Book

ENGINE TURNTABLES.

STATION.	DIAMETER OF TABLE.	TURNING CAPACITY.
Whitchurch	45 feet	All Engines L. and N.W. Table.
Wrexham	50 ,,	,,
Ellesmere	50 ,,	,,
Oswestry	45 feet 10 inches	,,
Welshpool	50 feet	,,
Moat Lane	50 ,,	,,
Llanidloes	45 ,,	,,
Builth Wells	45 ,,	,,
Talyllyn	...	Reverse through Loop
Brecon	50 feet	All Engines
Machynlleth	50 ,, _	,,
Aberystwyth	50 ,,	,,
Barmouth Junction	...	Reverse through Loop
Dolgelley	42 feet	All Engines (except Belpaire Pass.) G.W. Table.
Barmouth	45 ,,	All Engines
Afon Wen	45 ,,	,,

MID WALES SECTION.

INCLINE BETWEEN	LENGTH ABOUT	GRADIENT 1 IN	FALLING TOWARDS
Dolwen and Llanidloes	¾ mile	132	Dolwen
Llanidloes and Penpontbren	1 mile	75	Llanidloes
Llanidloes and Penpontbren	¼ mile	126	Llanidloes
Penpontbren and Tylwch	¾ mile	60	Penpontbren
Penpontbren and Tylwch	¼ mile	104	Penpontbren
Penpontbren, Tylwch, and Pantydwr	1½ miles	111	Penpontbren
Tylwch and Pantydwr	¾ mile	85	Tylwch
Tylwch and Pantydwr	1½ miles	77	Tylwch
Pantydwr and St. Harmons	¼ mile	114	St. Harmons
St. Harmons and Rhayader	¼ mile	80	Rhayader
St. Harmons and Rhayader	¼ mile	90	Rhayader
St. Harmons and Rhayader	¾ mile	90	Rhayader
St. Harmons and Rhayader	¼ mile	70	Rhayader
St. Harmons and Rhayader	¼ mile	75	Rhayader
Rhayader and Doldowlod	¼ mile	75	Rhayader
Rhayader and Doldowlod	1 mile	60	Doldowlod
Rhayader and Doldowlod	½ mile	75	Doldowlod
Rhayader and Doldowlod	¼ mile	112	Doldowlod
Doldowlod and Newbridge-on-Wye	¼ mile	75	Newbridge-on-Wye
Doldowlod and Newbridge-on-Wye	½ mile	75	Newbridge-on-Wye
Doldowlod and Newbridge-on-Wye	¼ mile	75	Doldowlod
Newbridge-on-Wye and Builth Road	¼ mile	75	Newbridge-on-Wye
Newbridge-on-Wye and Builth Road	¾ mile	100	Builth Road
Newbridge-on-Wye and Builth Road	¾ mile	100	Newbridge-on-Wye
Newbridge-on-Wye and Builth Road	1½ miles	95	Builth Road
Builth Wells and Builth Road	¼ mile	144	Builth Wells
Builth Road and Builth Wells	¼ mile	100	Builth Wells
Builth Wells and Aberedw	¼ mile	112	Builth Wells
Aberedw and Erwood	¼ mile	91	Erwood
Aberedw and Erwood	¼ mile	124	Erwood
Erwood and Boughrood and Llyswen	¼ mile	90	Boughrood & Llyswen
Erwood and Boughrood and Llyswen	¼ mile	75	Boughrood & Llyswen
Erwood and Boughrood and Llyswen	¼ mile	75	Boughrood & Llyswen
Three Cocks and Talgarth	¼ mile	140	Three Cocks
Three Cocks and Talgarth	¼ mile	75	Three Cocks
Three Cocks and Talgarth	¼ mile	90	Three Cocks
Three Cocks and Talgarth	¼ mile	140	Three Cocks
Talgarth and Trefeinon	¼ mile	75	Talgarth
Talgarth and Trefeinon	¼ mile	122	Talgarth
Trefeinon and Talyllyn	¼ mile	75	Trefeinon
Trefeinon and Talyllyn	½ mile	75	Trefeinon
Trefeinon and Talyllyn	½ mile	75	Trefeinon
Trefeinon and Talyllyn	½ mile	141	Trefeinon

Penpontbren Siding between Llanidloes and Tylwch.

When Trains stop at this Siding, the Guard must pin down not less than four wagon brakes, and sprag, on the Up journey, the front wagon with two sprags, and on the Down journey, the wagon next to the Brake Van, with two sprags, so that when the Engine is detached the Train may not move. The Guard will be responsible for working the points, also for the pinning down of the brakes of all wagons left in the Siding.

Glanyrafon Siding, between Tylwch and Pantydwr.

When Trains stop at this Siding, the Guard must pin down not less than four wagon brakes and sprag the wagon next to the Brake Van with two sprags, so that when the Engine is detached the Train may not move.

The Guards will be responsible for the locking of the gates and stop-block, and also for the pinning down of the brakes of all wagons left in the Siding.

Watt's Siding, between Doldowlod and Newbridge-on-Wye.

Guards leaving wagons in this Siding must pin down the Brakes and see that the Stop Block is locked before leaving.

Before commencing to load Timber at this Siding it will be necessary for two Flagmen to be stationed not less than 400 yards from the Siding, one on the Doldowlod side and one on the Newbridge-on-Wye side, to be provided with a red and green flag. They must bring all trains to a stand by the exhibition of a red flag, and call them on by the use of the green flag, after ascertaining that the Line is clear at the Siding.

Before commencing to load, the Timber Loaders must notify such intention to the Station Masters at Doldowlod and Newbridge-on-Wye respectively, who must caution the Drivers of all trains to look out for the Signals given by the Flagmen.

The Permanent Way Department will provide two Platelayers to act as Flagmen when required.

Thomas' Siding, between Newbridge-on-Wye and Builth Road.

Guards leaving wagons in this Siding must pin down the Brakes and see that the Stop Block is locked before leaving.

Llanelwedd Quarry Siding near Builth Wells.

This Siding will be shunted once daily between 10-45 and 11-30 a.m. Wagons for the Siding will be propelled from Builth Wells Station with a goods brake in front. The Shunter must see that the wagons left in the Siding are inside the catch points, after the shunting in the Siding is completed, and that the brakes are properly pinned down.

ENGINE WHISTLES

Station or Junction.	To or From.	Whistles.
LLANIDLOES, NORTH CABIN *Continued*	Up Sidings to and from Down Sidings	3 Crows
	Up Sidings to Up Main	1 Crow 2 Short
	Up Sidings to Down Main	5 Short
	Goods Yard to and from Neck ...	2 Crows 1 Long
	Goods Yard to and from Main ...	4 Short
	Down Main to and from Warehouse Sidings ...	1 Short 2 Crows
	Neck to and from Warehouse Siding	2 Long
RHAYADER.	Up and Down Main Line	1
	From Moat Lane end of Yard to and from Goods Shed	2 & 1 Crow
	From Moat Lane end of Yard to Up Line ...	3
	From Brecon end of Yard to Goods Shed	2
	From Brecon end of Yard to Up Line	2 & 2 Crows
	For Carriage Dock	1 & 1 Crow
	For Cross-over Road	4 Short
	From Up Main Line to North Neck ·	3 & 1 Crow

ENGINE WHISTLES—*continued.*

STATION OR JUNCTION.	TO OR FROM.	WHISTLES.
BUILTH ROAD LOOP.	For L. and N.W. Main Line	1
	To and from L. and N.W. Siding	2
	From Cambrian Siding	3
	To and from L. & N.W. Engine Shed Siding ...	4
BUILTH ROAD STATION.	Up and Down Trains to and from Station ...	1 Whistle
	Main Line to and from L. & N.W. Loop ...	2 Whistles
	From Neck to and from L. & N.W. Loop... ...	3 „
	From Neck to Cross-over Road	4 „
	To and from Bridge Siding	1 Whistle and 1 Crow
	From Up Loop to Neck	2 Whistles & 2 Crows
	For Cross-over Road	3 Whistles & 1 Crow
	To and from Coal Siding	2 Crows
BUILTH WELLS.	Up and Down Main Line	1
	To and from Main Line to Shed Road Brecon end of Yard	2
	To and from Shunting Neck Brecon end of Yard ...	3
	To and from Wall Siding	4
	To Cross-over Road from Up or Down Line ...	5
	To and from Up Main Line to Goods Shed Llanidloes end of Yard	1 & 1 Crow
	To and from Carriage Siding...	1 & 2 Crows
	To and from Carriage Dock	1 & 3 Crows
	To and from Permanent Way Siding Llanidloes end of Yard	1 & 4 Crows
THREE COCKS JUNCTION.	Up and Down Main Line	1
	To or from Hereford Line	2
	Down Midland Line to and from South Siding Neck	2 and 1 Crow
	To and from Up Main Line for East Shunting Neck	2 and 3 Crows.
	Cross-over from Up Midland to Back Siding ...	4 Short
	From Up Midland Line through compound to Down Line and *vice-versa*	6 „
	From East Shunting Neck to and from Weighing Machine	3 and 1 Crow
	From South Neck to and from Back Siding ...	1 and 2 Crows
TALGARTH.	Up and Down Main Line	1
	From Moat Lane end for Cross-over Road to and from Goods Shed	4
	From Cross-over Road to and from Down Line...	3
	From Down Line to and from Neck	2 and 2 Crows
	From Neck to and from Carriage Dock.	2 and 1 Crow